Germany

Germany

BY JEAN F. BLASHFIELD

Enchantment of the World
Second Series

Children's Press®

A Division of Scholastic Inc.

NEW YORK   TORONTO   LONDON   AUCKLAND   SYDNEY
MEXICO CITY   NEW DELHI   HONG KONG
DANBURY, CONNECTICUT

Frontispiece: Berchtesgaden beer hall

Consultant: Heidi Rauscher Tilghman, University of Washington, Seattle

Please note: All statistics are as up-to-date as possible at the time of publication.

Book production by Herman Adler Design

Library of Congress Cataloging-in-Publication Data

Blashfield, Jean F.
 Germany / by Jean F. Blashfield.
   p. cm. — (Enchantment of the world. Second series)
 Includes bibliographical references and index.
 ISBN 0-516-22376-3
 1. Germany—Juvenile literature. [1. Germany.] I. Title. II. Series.
DD17 .B53 2003
943—dc21   2001008503

Acknowledgments

The author gratefully thanks the German National Tourist Office; the State Historical Society of Wisconsin; the University of Wisconsin–Madison; the University of Wisconsin–Whitewater; and Hedburg Library, Janesville, Wisconsin. And thanks to the German people for their hospitality.

Contents

Cover photo:
Berchtesgaden,
Bavaria

CHAPTER

Brandenburg Gate

Folk dancers

A New Germany

O<small>N</small> J<small>UNE</small> 26, 1963, U<small>NITED</small> S<small>TATES</small> <small>PRESIDENT</small> J<small>OHN</small> F. Kennedy visited the German city of West Berlin. As a result of World War II, the city had been cut off from the Western world since 1945. Standing in front of the Schöneberg Town Hall, he spoke to a large crowd: "There are some who say communism is the wave of the future. Let them come to Berlin. All free men, wherever they may live, are citizens of Berlin, and, therefore, as a free man, I take pride in the words *'Ich bin ein Berliner.'*"

Opposite: **Berliners join hands on top of the Berlin Wall to celebrate the opening of East–West German borders on November 10, 1989.**

President Kennedy pledged his support to West Berlin against communist threats.

When the U.S. president said "I am a citizen of Berlin," he was telling the world that free people were not forgetting the beleaguered city that had been divided in two—half communist and half capitalist—as a result of World War II. President Kennedy did not live to see Berlin united once again. He was assassinated twenty-seven years before that happened. Today, however, he might again have said, *"Ich bin ein Berliner."* The world has watched as the once-divided city—and the German nation—thrives again in unity.

The official name of Germany is the Federal Republic of Germany, or *Bundesrepublik Deutschland.* Today, that is the name of the entire country. From 1949 to 1990, that name was reserved for what was called West Germany. The nation called East Germany was the German Democratic Republic, often shortened to the GDR.

Germany is now the wealthiest and most populous nation in western Europe. It lies at the center of the continent and at the crossroads of Europe's business and cultural worlds. It also serves as the connection between western Europe and eastern Europe, as well as between Scandinavia and the Mediterranean world.

Germany has been at the center of change for hundreds of years. One important change was brought about by a German named Johannes Gutenberg. A resident of the town of Mainz in the 1450s, Gutenberg had an idea for making printing easier. Books had been copied by hand for centuries. They had even been printed by carving the words of a page into a smooth slab of wood.

A New Germany **11**

Geopolitical map
of Germany

GERMANY

- Cities of over 500,000 people
- Smaller cities and towns

0 — 60 miles
0 — 90 kilometers

National Parks

Ⓐ Bavarian Forest
Ⓑ Berchtesgaden
Ⓒ Bodden
Ⓓ Harz
Ⓔ Jasmund
Ⓕ Lauren Lakes Nature Reserve
Ⓖ Müritz
Ⓗ Schleswig-Holstein

DENMARK

Baltic Sea

North Sea

NETHERLANDS

POLAND

CZECH REPUBLIC

AUSTRIA

FRANCE

SWITZERLAND

Schleswig
Kiel
Fehmarn I.
Hiddensee I.
Ⓒ
Ⓔ Rügen I.
Ⓗ
Kiel Canal
Wattenmeer
Lübeck
Ⓕ Schwerin
Ⓖ
Hamburg
Bremen
Weser R.
Elbe R.
Oder R.
Aller R.
Former division of East and West Germany
Berlin
Mittleland Canal
Hanover
Braunschweig
Ⓓ
Magdeburg
Potsdam
Spree R.
Wittenberg
Münster
Eisleben
Leipzig
Ruhr R.
Essen
Kassel
Marbach
Dortmund
Eder R.
Erfurt
Dresden
Elberfield
Düsseldorf
Eisenach
Hohenstein-Ernstthal
Aachen
Cologne
Werra R.
Bonn
Frankfurt
Bayreuth
Mainz
Main R.
Bingen
Worms
Nürnberg
Mannheim
Heidelberg
Ⓐ
Ludwigshafen
Hanau
Leimen
Stuttgart
Danube R.
Rhine R.
Baden-Baden
Ulm
Augsburg
Isar R.
Lech R.
Dachau
Munich
Bodensee
Oberammergau
Ⓑ
Mittenwald
Garmisch-Partinkirchen

N
W E
S

Germany

Understanding Terms

In reading this book you will need to understand several different terms to follow the history of Germany in the last decades.

East refers to East Germany, or the German Democratic Republic, which existed from 1949 to 1989. *East* also refers to the entire communist world, most of which was in eastern Europe and Asia. GDR stands for the German Democratic Republic. *Eastern Germany* means East Germany after reunification; *Western Germany* means West Germany after reunification.

West refers to West Germany, or the Federal Republic of Germany from 1949 to 1990. It also refers to the noncommunist world of Europe and the Americas.

In this book, *West Germany* is always used for the Federal Republic of Germany during the period of division.

Berlin Wall refers to the actual wall that was built in 1961 by the Soviet government of East Germany to separate East Berlin from West Berlin. It also symbolizes the separation of East and West.

Place names are generally given in their English version except the first time. For example, we use the name Cologne for the city called *Köln* in German.

One of the most common phrases in Germany and throughout this book is "the war." It refers to World War II (1939–1945), which determined events that have happened to the nation since then.

Gutenberg thought that it would be easier to create individual letters by engraving them on tiny blocks of steel. The indented letters would be pushed against a softer metal. That softer metal formed letters that were raised and backward. Ink was then rolled across the surface of the metal. When paper was laid on the inked surface, the inked impression was a correctly reading page of type. The letters that were used would then be taken from their frame and used again to make new words for another printing. Printing became an important activity in towns all over Europe. For the first time, information could be widely spread.

From Seas to Alps

ERMANY IS LOCATED IN A REGION THAT IS USUALLY called Central Europe. It has been central to European history for centuries. History is not all that Germany has to offer. It has a magnificent landscape of beautiful forests, enchanting rivers, stunning mountains, and coastlines.

Germany measures 137,846 square miles (356,994 square kilometers), including the islands in the North and Baltic Seas. This is slightly smaller than the state of Montana. Germany has been settled for so long, and has so many cities, towns, and roads, that few places remain with their original landscape.

Germany is surrounded by nine countries. To the north along the peninsula called Jutland, which lies between the North Sea and the Baltic Sea, is Denmark. To the west are France, the Netherlands, Belgium, Luxembourg, and France. Switzerland and Austria lie to the south. The Czech Republic and Poland lie to the east.

The distance around the borders is 2,248 miles (3,618 kilometers). Germany's longest single border is with Austria— 487 miles (784 km). Its shortest is

Opposite: **Germany's scenic areas include mountains, forests, and lakes as well as rugged coastlines and winding rivers.**

Green forested hills are dwarfed by the majestic mountains of Bavaria.

The elevation of Germany's land rises from the north toward the south, where it meets the Alps. Its lowest point is Freepsum Lake, which has an elevation of 6.5 feet (2 meters) below sea level. Its highest point is Zugspitze, a mountain peak that reaches 9,721 feet (2,963 m) in the Bavarian Alps far to the south. A cable car takes visitors to the top of the mountain.

with Denmark, only 42 miles (68 km). The longest distance north to south is 540 miles (870 km). From west to east, it is 398 miles (641 km).

Politically, the land is divided into sixteen states, called Länder. Three of the Länder are cities—Berlin, Hamburg, and Bremen. Of the larger Länder, Bavaria (*Bayern*) is the largest in area and Thuringia (*Thüringen*) is the smallest, not counting the three city-states.

The Coast and the Islands

In the north, on each side of the Jutland Peninsula, is Germany's only seacoast. The coastline on these two seas totals 1,484 miles (2,388 km). The main German islands in the North Sea are the East Frisian Islands and most of the North Frisian Islands. (The West Frisian Islands belong to the Netherlands, and some of the North Frisian Islands belong to Denmark.) They are all quite low in elevation.

Coastline of the Jutland Peninsula

Between the German groups of islands, in the bay called the Helgoland Bight, is another North Frisian Island, called Helgoland. This island was owned by Britain in the 1800s, but that nation traded it for Zanzibar in Africa in 1890. In both world wars Helgoland was an important military installation. Today it is a tourist resort.

On the other side of Jutland, in the Baltic Sea, are the islands of Rügen, Hiddensee, and Fehmarn. Rügen is the largest German island. It is about 32 miles (51 km) long. These islands are very different from the Frisians. They are high and rocky and have spectacular chalk cliffs. Sometimes the cliffs are broken by deep indentations made by the sea. Tiny Jasmund National Park is located on Rügen.

Natural chalk formation on Rügen Island

Rising from North to South

From the cold waters of the North Sea and the Baltic Sea, the German land rises toward the Alps Mountains. They lie far to the south by Switzerland.

Between the Frisian Islands and the mainland, the water is very shallow, and when the tide is out, the land is exposed as mud flats. The adjacent mainland is part of the North German Lowland, which occupies the northern third of the country. The land is so low that tidal water flows way up into the land. Much of this entire northern third is wetland, though some of it has been drained for agriculture.

The Rhine River gently winds its way past Burg Katz Castle in the Rhine Valley.

Nowhere is the North German Lowland more than 656 feet (200 m) in elevation, but that elevation can create beautiful Scandinavian-like fjords—steep-sided valleys filled by water from the sea. Glaciers that retreated 10,000 years ago left the land flat, with many small rivers and marshes that are linked by canals.

The southern part of the North German Lowland is an important, fertile agricultural area. The Mittelland Canal, begun in 1905, is 199 miles (320 km) long and crosses the middle of Germany. Its barge traffic carries agricultural products, coal, and iron.

To the south lies the Central Upland Region. It is a mixed bag of hills, small upland plains, and rough terrain. It averages a little more than 3,300 feet (1,006 m) in elevation. The highest point of this region is in the Harz Mountains, not far west of Berlin. Harz National Park contains Brocken, a mountain that reaches 3,747 feet (1,142 m). The Rhine (*Rhein*) and the Mosel River Valleys make deep and beautiful indentations in the uplands.

The region usually called Southern Germany divides the Central Uplands from the Alps Mountains. This is a fairly rough region of high valleys. Small ranges of mountains, such as the Jura, stretch into the area from France and Switzerland. Above the Danube River is a tableland, or plateau, that rises toward the Alps Mountains. This is a colorful region of lakes, hills, moors, and beautiful forests.

The Alps region offers stunning views of mountains, forests, and lakes.

The Alps Mountains themselves lie at the southern end of Germany along the border of Bavaria. These are Germany's most striking mountains, though Germany can claim only the smallest portion of the Alps. This spectacular mountain range is shared with Italy, France, Switzerland, Austria, and Slovenia.

The Bavarian Alps may be small, but they possess an important world ski area in Garmisch-Partenkirchen. The Winter Games of the Olympics were held here in 1936. The nearby village of Mittenwald has been a center of the violin-making arts for centuries.

The Bavarian Alpine area called Berchtesgaden is one of the most beautiful places in the country. Today, much of it is a national park featuring the long clear lake called Königssee. Germany's second-highest mountain, Watzmann, is 8,901 feet (2,713 m) high and located there.

The Königssee as seen from Jenner Mountain in Berchtesgaden

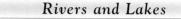

The primary rivers of Germany flow northward into the North or the Baltic Sea. The Rhine, the Weser, and the Elbe are among these. Two of the largest industrial cities are located on rivers wide and deep enough for commercial shipping to reach them. They are Bremen, on the Weser, and Hamburg, on the Elbe.

The Rhine, in the far west, rises in the Alps Mountains of Switzerland and heads through Germany also toward the North Sea, which it reaches through the Netherlands. Though it is more than 800 miles (1,287 km) long, only 542 miles (872 km) of the Rhine flow through Germany. Alongside the Black Forest in the south, the Rhine forms part of the border between France and Germany.

When the Rhine first rises in Switzerland, it travels through Germany's largest lake, *Bodensee*—known to English speakers as Lake Constance. More than half of Lake Constance is in Germany; the remainder is in Switzerland and Austria.

Bodensee, Germany's largest lake, with the Swiss Alps in the background.

In the north, between Berlin and the Baltic, lies a series of lakes within Müritz National Park. The area is often called the Mecklenburg Lake District. It's been estimated to include more than 1,000 lakes of varying sizes. The largest is Müritz itself, which is Germany's second-largest lake.

The Lorelei Rock

At the narrowest point in the Rhine River, near Cologne, is a mighty rock where, myth says, the beautiful maiden Lorelei lives. She lures sailors and fishers to their deaths with her enchanting singing. What the sailors of old didn't know was that a whirlpool forms around the rock. It could trap a ship with or without a mythological maiden.

Along the cliffs above the Rhine are the romantic-looking ruins of several castles built long ago by feudal overlords. They captured ships trapped by the natural currents and took the goods they were carrying, gradually becoming wealthy. This part of the river is an important site on the Rhine River boat tours that sail to Cologne.

An exception to the northward flow of rivers is the famed Danube, the second-largest river in Europe. It rises in the Black Forest, crosses Bavaria, and then enters Austria, where it heads toward the Black Sea. The Danube's importance is to Austrians what the Rhine's is to Germans.

Germany's Geographical Features

Area: 137,846 square miles (356,994 sq km)

Highest Elevation: Zugspitze, in the Bavarian Alps, 9,721 feet (2,963 m) above sea level

Lowest Elevation: Freepsum Lake, 6.5 feet (2 m) below sea level

Longest River: Rhine River, 542 miles (872 km) through Germany

Largest Lake: Lake Constance (*Bodensee*), 208 square miles (539 sq km)

Coastline: 1,484 miles (2,388 km)

Longest Shared Border: 487 miles (784 km) with Austria

Greatest Distance North to South: 540 miles (870 km)

Greatest Distance East to West: 398 miles (641 km)

Largest City (2000 est.): Berlin, 3,458,763

Climate

The climate in northwestern Germany tends to be moderate all year round. Though it is as far north as Canada's Hudson Bay, it has an average year-round temperature of 50° Fahrenheit (10° Celsius). The extremes that its latitude could bring, are softened by the effects of the Gulf Stream. This ocean current's warm water pours around Great Britain and into the North Sea.

This moderating warmth does not reach the southern and eastern parts of the country. Those parts, deep within the European continent, experience a continental climate, meaning that summers are hot and winters are cold.

Precipitation is fairly even all year long. The western part of Germany, which is closer to the Atlantic Ocean, gets more rainfall each year than the eastern part.

Winters are variable, depending on which air masses control the weather. Warmer and wet weather comes from the Atlantic. Colder, drier air comes from the northeast. Average winter temperatures range between 35°F (1°C) in low-lying areas and 21°F (–6°C) in the mountains.

Summers can be just as variable, with long, damp summer days under cloud-covered skies, or weeks of sunshine, with drought conditions. Average July temperatures are between 64°F (17.8°C) in low-lying regions and 68°F (20°C) in the southern alpine valleys.

The *Föhn*, or foehn, is a wind that occurs in the fall over the alpine area. Similar to the chinook in North America, it is a dry wind that comes from the east, bringing clear skies and pleasantly cool weather.

Looking at Germany's Cities

Hamburg, located on the Elbe River in northern Germany, is the country's second-largest city. This city grew around Hammaburg Castle during the 830s. A major European port, Hamburg is known for ship-building and oil refining. More recently, it also has become known as a publishing center. The city houses the University of Hamburg, with about 42,000 students.

Munich, Germany's third-largest city, is located on the Isar River in the south. Founded about 1158 on the site of a monastery, its name means "monk settlement." Munich is a center of trade, high-tech and media industries, and culture. Leading manufactured products include precision instruments, automobiles, and beer. The city is home to the University of Munich, the Glyptothek Museum, and the BMW Museum.

Cologne (below), Germany's fourth-largest city, is located on the Rhine River in the western state of North Rhine-Westphalia. Settled by Julius Caesar about 50 B.C., the city was named Colonia Claudia Ara Agrippinensis in A.D. 50 for Agrippina, the wife of the emperor Claudius. Today, Cologne is an important river port and banking center. Main industries are chemicals and *eau de cologne* (fragrances). The city has many museums and beautiful churches, including the Roman-Germanic Museum and the famous Cologne Cathedral.

Frankfurt am Main (above), located on the Main River, is Germany's fifth-largest city. By the first century A.D., Frankfurt was a Roman military settlement. It gained importance as a trading center during the time of Charlemagne, who was king around 800. Today, Frankfurt is a main financial and transportation center in Germany. The Bundesbank, the European Central Bank, and Germany's main stock market are located in this city. Frankfurt is also known for its annual international book fair.

From Seas to Alps **25**

Wildlife
and Forests

Approximately 30 percent of Germany's land is covered by forest, making timber one of its natural resources. Most of the original forests of oak and other hardwoods of northern Germany were cut down hundreds of years ago for firewood and building materials. The land once occupied by them was gradually covered by sandy soil in which trees of little, if any, value grew. In the last century, however, the land has been fertilized and softwood forests, primarily pine trees, have been planted. Throughout Germany, forests have been badly damaged by too many years of acid rain caused by industrial pollution.

The Black Forest, at the southwestern corner of the country, is called "black" because its evergreen trees are so dark that they look black. Cuckoo clocks are produced in this region of Germany.

The Bavarian Forest, on the eastern side of Bavaria, is a national park. It joins up with the Bohemian Forest in the Czech Republic. Together these forests make the largest forested area in Europe.

Opposite: **Cows graze in lush pastures in the Black Forest.**

The dark, blackish evergreens of the Black Forest

The watery world of northern Germany and the Jutland Pensinula provides wonderful sanctuaries for birds migrating between the Mediterranean and the Arctic. There are three low-lying national parks in this region, called the *Wattenmeer* (Wadden Sea). Actually, they are one single large park, but because they are located in three separate states, they are regarded as three separate parks. They total 3,088 square miles (7,998 sq km). Schleswig-Holstein at 1,050 miles (2,721 sq km) is the largest, made up of tidal flats where numerous birds feed.

Bodden National Park in West Pomerania lies along the Baltic Sea coast. It includes 311 square miles (805 sq km) of islands, peninsulas, and sand dunes. It is one of the few natural areas remaining in Germany. Birds threatened elsewhere

The sun rises over the Oder River wetlands, where birds and other animals can be found.

A spider builds its web on a fly orchid.

are found in abundance along the estuaries of the coastal rivers. This is particularly true of Unteres Odertal, which is an international park, not a national one, because it is partly in Germany and partly in Poland. Primarily wetlands around the Oder River, it is home to many birds and other rare species.

Cranes and storks are regular residents of the beautiful lake-filled nature preserve called *Lauenburgische Seen* found east of Hamburg. Various orchids and insect-eating plants grow in the wetlands of the area.

The Storks of Germany

White storks are regarded throughout Europe as good luck. Perhaps that's why they were the transport for newborn babies, according to tales told to children. This large bird is white on its chest, neck, and head, and black elsewhere. It stands about 3 to 4 feet (90 to 120 cm) tall. Storks have always nested high on chimney tops or in trees in Europe after spending the winters in Africa. These wonderful birds are almost gone now because they are attracted to undrained land, and little of that is left. Villages that work to attract storks earn the title of European Stork Village.

The moorlands around the Mecklenburg Lake District are breeding grounds for species of cranes and ospreys. Both Mecklenburg and Müritz National Park protect sea eagles, which are large, heavy eagles that nest along rocky heights.

Once known for its bears and wolves, Germany now lacks these animals except in zoos. However, some wolves occasionally venture into eastern Germany from countries farther east.

Wild boars roam the woods of Bavaria, especially in the Hass Mountains. The number of these potentially dangerous tusked pigs grew alarmingly after the war, but legalized hunting has gradually reduced their number again.

Wild boar

In the Alps, two spectacular mountain members of the sheep and goat family—chamois and ibex—are protected. The Alpine chamois is a goatlike animal with elastic hoofs that can bend and twist with the rocky surface of its high-mountain habitat. Male chamois generally live isolated lives, while the females live in herds. Ibex, which have long curved horns, live in herds.

Smaller mammals such as beaver and mink are threatened or endangered throughout Europe. Their habitats are being protected.

The goatlike chamois lives a protected life in the Alps.

German Cattle

A number of cattle breeds have been developed in Germany. Often they originated elsewhere. The Holstein, for example, originated in the Netherlands but was developed in Germany. It is one of the most popular breeds in the world for dairy cattle. More recently the Swiss Simmental and the German Angus have been bred in Germany. One of the smallest breeds of cattle in central Europe is the Hinterwald (pictured), which lives in the Black Forest, where it thrives on the steep slopes of mountains.

Caring for the Environment

West Germans became actively involved in recycling, pollution control, and other aspects of tending the Earth in the 1960s and 1970s. Among the first projects undertaken was cleaning up the main industrial rivers. Several of them, including parts of the Rhine and the Ruhr, had no life in them because chemical waste had been dumped in them for so long. Today, they have been cleaned up and even support fish life once more.

West Germans were proud of the progress they had made. When the Berlin Wall came down, it was a shock to discover that East Germany had continued to abuse the environment

Pollution is high in eastern Germany, although the government has taken steps to keep it under control.

for decades. This misuse had been a conscious decision on the part of the East German government because growth of the economy was more important to them than the environment.

Almost one-third of East German homes had no plumbing that connected to a sewage system. Instead, human waste went directly into rivers and lakes. More than half of eastern Germany's water sources are still too polluted for use, and more than half of the remainder must be heavily treated for the water to be drinkable.

West Germany itself had contributed to the environmental conditions in East Germany. The GDR had been paid by West Germany to accept huge mountains of its trash, and instead of being disposed of in safe landfills, it was just dumped.

Today the environment is a concern throughout the country. Formed in 1979, the Green political party, which focuses on the environment, won seats in the West German legislature right away. The Green Party will probably be part of any coalition of political parties agreeing to work together in the government in the near future.

It has not been possible to improve everything all at once in eastern Germany. Gradually, steps are being taken to tackle each aspect of environmental concern. Within sight are clean air and water, and improved habitats for wildlife.

German Work Dogs

German shepherds (above)—also known as Alsatians, from the French-German region called Alsace—were originally bred for their herding ability. They often appear to lead sheep instead of chasing them, but they continually look back to see if the sheep—or their human owners—are following nicely. Shepherds are fairly large dogs with tan-and-black hair. Calm, even-tempered dogs, they are often trained as Seeing Eye dogs to lead the blind. In recent years, eastern Germany bred its own bloodlines that emphasize work-ing. The breed closest to the original German shepherd is called the Altdeutscher Hütehund. It is all black.

The German shorthaired pointer (right) is a popular sporting dog that can be the solid dark-reddish color usually called liver, or can have splotches of liver and white. It was developed after the 1700s, when guns had acquired enough accuracy for a hunter to take down birds in flight. The pointers can locate the downed birds and bring them back to the hunter.

The Making of a New Germany

TRIBES OF PEOPLE SETTLED IN THE REGION NORTH OF THE Italian boot starting about 500 B.C. These peoples called themselves by such names as Sicambri, Bructeri, Marsi, and Cherusci. In later centuries, though, the people were called Germanic, after the language of one of the tribes. The region they occupied came to be called Germania.

The Roman Empire attempted to control Germania, but it won and lost the region several times. Julius Caesar neglected Germania because he thought that unicorns and other alarming beasts lived in its dense forests. One battle with the Romans, in A.D. 9, produced the first German hero, a prince named Arminius. He defeated three Roman legions near today's Bielefeld.

In A.D. 98, the Roman historian Tacitus wrote a book called *Germania*. He described the peoples who lived along the Rhine River in the far reaches of the Roman Empire as brave, strong, and moral, as well as ill-mannered and greedy. He also described them as a "pure-blooded people" descended from one tribe. This was an idea that would appeal to many Germans eighteen centuries later.

The last Roman emperor, Romulus Augustus, was forced to give up the throne

Opposite: **Bavarians battle for the imperial throne in Germany's early days *(top)*; coronation of German king Lothair III *(bottom)* in 1133.**

Arminius led Germanic tribes to victory against the Roman legions in A.D. 9.

in 476 by Germanic troops coming into Rome from the north. The Germanic tribes began to spread throughout Europe, gradually forming the basis of new peoples in Italy, Britain, France, and Germany.

In about the 700s, Latin—and the Romance languages that derive from it—was the major language throughout much of Europe. The term *deutsch* began to be applied to those people who spoke other languages. The location where these people lived was called *Deutschland*, which is what the Germans call Germany today.

Charlemagne's Holy Empire

Throughout the years after the fall of the Roman Empire, Christianity spread in Europe, often by the work of wandering monks from Britain and Ireland. The most powerful people were the Franks, who had taken from the Romans those regions that later became France, Belgium, and western Germany. Strongest of all the leaders in the 700s and early 800s was the Frankish king Charles the Great, known as Charlemagne (742–814). Many historians say that German history starts with Charlemagne.

Charlemagne gathered many of the small kingdoms of northern Europe, such as Bavaria, Saxony, Thuringia, Frisia, and Hesse, into one supernation. He united for the first time some of the regions that today are states, or *Länder*, of Germany.

In 774, Charlemagne's troops captured the region of Italy called Lombardy, which had been attacking the Catholic

Charlemagne, king of the Franks and Holy Roman emperor

Central Danzig was under control of the Hanseatic League.

Church's headquarters in Rome. Six years later, in 800, the pope, who was head of the Catholic Church, crowned Charlemagne emperor for that rescue. Charlemagne's empire came to be called the Holy Roman Empire.

The territory of Charlemagne's empire did not remain the same for long because he was not followed by leaders that had his powerful personality. Numerous other kings, princes, and even emperors ruled over some or all of the territory at one time or another. Throughout these years the largest of the kingdoms were Saxony, Franconia, Swabia, and Bavaria.

The emperor shared power with the leaders of those states making up the empire. Royal figures that headed the individual states were sometimes called elector princes because they participated in the election of a new emperor.

Businessmen grew to be powerful people during the coming centuries. The merchants of the major seaport cities of northern Germany organized to protect their cities, ships, and goods as they traded throughout the Baltic and Atlantic ports. They called themselves the Hanseatic League, from *hansa*, which meant "company of merchants." Their home cities, such as Hamburg, Bremen, Lübeck, and Cologne, as well as the ones they traded with, came to be called Hanseatic ports. All Hanseatic ports were protected by the league's own troops.

Martin Luther preaching to a small congregation.

A Religious Revolution

In the sixteenth century, some territories of the Holy Roman Empire began claiming their own nationhood because of a new kind of revolution. Led by a German priest named Martin Luther, people began to protest against the Catholic Church in Rome. This movement is called the Reformation. They said that following the pope was not the only way to be a Christian. These people came to be called Protestants.

With the spread of Protestantism, the emperor of the Holy Roman Empire stopped being crowned by the pope. The empire was no longer "holy," though the name was not dropped until 1806, when French dictator Napoléon I destroyed it. Voltaire, a French writer and philospher at that time, said of the Holy Roman Empire that it was "neither holy, nor Roman, nor an empire."

For a number of years, religious wars took place among the various German states—Catholics versus Protestants (or Lutherans, as they were derogatorily called). Finally, in 1555, the Diet, the parliament of the Holy Roman Empire, decreed the Peace of Augsburg. By it, freedom of religion was established, and the various states agreed not to fight with one another for religious reasons.

Rome had no intention of letting Germany go to the "protestors." A movement of the Catholic faithful called the Counter-Reformation began. This was an attempt to regroup and reverse the spread of Protestantism. The result was the Thirty Years' War, which lasted from 1618 to1648. Those countries that supported the Protestants became heavily Protestant. Those that supported the Catholics became heavily Catholic.

Thirty Years' War battle scene

The Holy Roman Empire ceased to exist on August 6, 1806. The emperor, Francis II, gave up his crown in the face of defeat by the French emperor Napoléon Bonaparte. Thirty-four separate German states became part of a Confederation of the Rhine, created by Napoléon.

The short-lived confederation was dissolved by November 1813, though it was almost two more years before Napoléon was finally defeated at the Battle of Waterloo in June 1815. Very quickly, an international meeting, called the Congress of Vienna, was assembled to decide the shape of post-Napoleonic Europe.

The most important powers were those that had defeated Napoléon—England, Russia, and the most powerful of the German states, Austria and Prussia. These countries had the task of deciding how to keep France from causing more trouble, as it had on and off for 200 years. The only structure that could do this was a strong and stable unified Germany next door. The congress, with the Treaty of Vienna, created a new German Confederation. However, it had no power because it had no central

The leaders of Europe debate during the Congress of Vienna.

government holding its more than forty member-states together.

Prussia was doubled in size when it was given several other regions to control. During the following decades, as industry was developed in Germany, most industrial growth took place along the northern Rhine, which Prussia controlled.

German history became the struggle between Prussia, represented by the Hohenzollern family, whose lands were primarily in the north, and

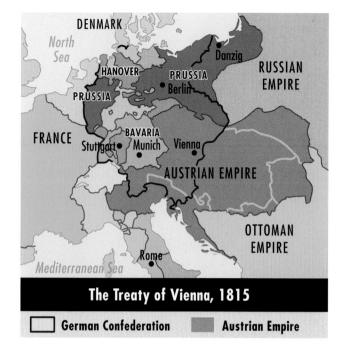

The Treaty of Vienna, 1815

German Confederation   Austrian Empire

Austria, as represented by the Habsburg family, whose land was primarily in the south, including Italy. Neither wanted a strong, unified Germany because each wanted to control it. Between these two German powers lay a group of middle-sized states that just tried to stay out of the way of trouble.

Many people favored the romantic notion of a single nation to be made of the area in which German was spoken. In 1848, in many of the states, liberals were elected to their local governments in a rebellion against the various monarchies. They sent delegates to an assembly in Frankfurt, where the parliament they formed agreed to take over the governments of the region. However, this new government had no money and no authority. Nor could it gain the recognition of the major foreign powers. Clearly, this new government—Germany's first real attempt at a republic—was not going to work.

The Beginning of Communism

A German journalist from Trier named Karl Marx lived in Paris, France, and Brussels, Belgium, in the 1840s. There he studied the ideas of Stuttgart-born philosopher Georg Hegel and became friends with another German, Friedrich Engels. Engels had been disturbed by the sight of great poverty among the working class of Manchester in England. Together, Marx and Engels (pictured) wrote a short pamphlet called the *Communist Manifesto*, which was published in 1848. It called for the destruction of *capitalism*, which is private ownership of industry. In its place, all means of production would be owned by the workers themselves—the *proletariat*. Marx believed that a society consisting of various classes would inevitably disappear.

Many people preferred a republic. They took to the streets, trying to work up enthusiasm. Troops from Prussia were able to crush this revolution. As a result, however, almost a million German people left Europe for the United States.

Prussian leader prince Otto von Bismarck gradually pulled together several northern German-speaking principalities, kingdoms, and city-states to create—by a combination of diplomacy and several small wars—a new German nation. It was called the North German Confederation. At its head was Wilhelm I, the king of Prussia.

By winning still other small wars, the confederation attracted some southern kingdoms. After a war against France in 1871, the confederation became the German Empire. At its head was Wilhelm, who became the first German *kaiser* (caesar, or king). Bismarck, as prime minister of Prussia, became the first German chancellor, or chief minister of state.

Two important Germanic peoples were left out of the confederation. Switzerland proceeded to go its own way, but Austria was so big and so important that there would continue to be wars between it and the German Empire for decades. Sometimes these wars would involve all of Europe—indeed, the world.

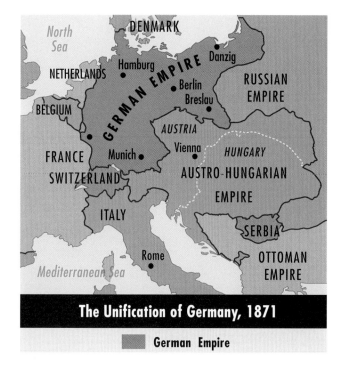

The Unification of Germany, 1871

■ German Empire

The Great War

Otto von Bismarck kept the new German Empire together. In 1890, the new kaiser, Wilhelm II, who was the grandson of Britain's Queen Victoria, dismissed Bismarck from office. Wilhelm took over Germany's policies himself. Those policies included building a large military, especially a huge navy. He gradually angered all of Germany's neighbors, especially Russia, France, and Britain.

Many other sparks of war were being ignited by conflicts among European states. The whole of Europe was ready to explode into war. It did so on June 28, 1914, when the heir to the throne of Austria, Archduke Francis Ferdinand, was killed

The assassination of Archduke Francis Ferdinand

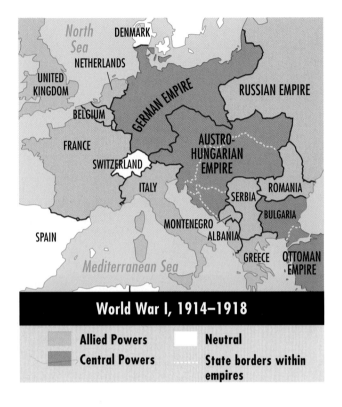

World War I, 1914–1918

Allied Powers   Neutral

Central Powers   State borders within empires

by a Serbian nationalist named Gavrilo Princip, from Bosnia. War was declared on August 1, and other countries joined in days. The nations of Europe quickly sided with either Austria or Serbia, basically pitting Germany (on the side of the Austrians) against Russia (on the side of the Serbs). Many Germans saw the war as a chance for Germany—with its strong new military—to emerge as the most powerful of Europe's nations.

The Great War lasted four years. (It wasn't called World War I until there was a World War II.) France and England entered the fray, and then the United States joined in 1917. Finally, on November 11, 1918, the signing of an armistice, or truce, ended the war. The Treaty of Versailles, signed in June 1919, dealt very harshly with Germany. Much German land was taken away and given to France, Belgium, Poland, and Denmark.

Two days before the war ended, the German chancellor resigned. In the following confusion, a leader of the Social Democratic party, Philipp Scheidemann, declared to the crowd around the Reichstag (the legislature building) that there was a new republican government. This became the Weimar Republic, since the Constitution was drafted in the town of Weimar.

More than 1.6 million Germans died as a result of World War I. The punishing Treaty of Versailles left those who survived poverty-stricken and increasingly angry. People had to use baskets to carry all the worthless currency needed just to buy a loaf of bread. The Weimar Republic was helpless, so the people looked to any political leader who would promise them a better future. Adolf Hitler of the National Socialist German Workers' (Nazi) Party became that leader.

Children hoping for food in Munich during the severe economic crisis following World War I.

Adolf Hitler: The Man Who Changed the World

A boy named Adolf Hitler was born April 20, 1889, in Braunau-am-Inn, Austria. His father's harshness turned the boy into a bully. When Adolf was a teenager, his parents died. For a while the young man, who had wanted to be an artist, lived homeless on the streets of Vienna. There he picked up harsh attitudes toward Jews, although he had several Jewish friends. He also acquired a fascination with politics. He gradually came to blame the Jews for the various humiliations he suffered on the streets. He found comfort in thinking that he and all "pure" Germans were superior to Jews and other peoples.

Just before World War I began, the young man moved to Munich, in Bavaria. There he proudly joined the Bavarian Army, which fought alongside the German Army. He was devastated when Germany was defeated by the Allied nations. He became angry as he saw his beloved adopted country failing to recover from defeat.

Hitler joined the tiny German Workers' Party and quickly became leader of the organization. He learned to speak in public and, gradually, to hold a crowd in the palm of his hand with his impassioned words. He gave his audiences someone to blame for all their troubles—he said that Jews were benefiting from the hardships his audience experienced.

The party—and Hitler's influence—grew. He changed the name of the party to the National Socialist German Workers' Party, which was quickly shortened to the Nazi Party. Many of the people who joined were thugs who gladly used violence.

In November 1923, he and his followers led an uprising and attempted to form a new government.

It failed, and Hitler was sent to prison. While locked up for a year, he wrote *Mein Kampf* (*My Struggle*), which told his story and explained his beliefs. It laid out his bloody plan for Germans to overwhelm all Jews and for Germany to become a powerful nation.

Year by year, the Nazi Party and Hitler himself became more powerful. He built a personal army of violent men willing to do anything to help him gain power. In 1933, Paul von Hindenburg, the president of the Weimar Republic, was forced to accept Hitler as his chancellor.

Hitler was finally in control. Germany—and ultimately Europe—were his to command as he willed. His will led, beginning in 1939, to World War II, the murders of millions of Jews and others, as well as the deaths of millions of soldiers the world over.

On April 30, 1945, war had been raging in Europe for almost six years. It was clear that once again the Germans were defeated. Adolf Hitler and his wife, Eva Braun, committed suicide in his underground bunker in Berlin.

Over the next few years, Hitler's influence grew. Then, in 1930, elections put Nazis into the Reichstag (the legislature) in large numbers. By 1933, their power was great enough to force Hindenburg, the president of the failing republic, to name Hitler chancellor. In August 1934, Hindenburg died. Hitler combined the offices of president and chancellor and took the title of *Führer*, meaning "leader" of the Third Reich. Firmly in control, he had his political opponents executed. Soon almost no one protested.

The "Final Solution"

The Nazis used the term *Aryan* to mean a person of pure Nordic, blond, blue-eyed heritage. Their powerful publicity machine focused blame for the problems of the nation on non-Aryans, especially Jews, who made up less than 1 percent of Germany's population.

A devastated synagogue from the night of glass.

Nazi soldiers were told to go ahead and terrorize any Jews they saw. Many Jews thought that the terror would pass, and they stayed in Germany. Others hurriedly took what money they had and fled the country.

On November 9, 1938, in one dramatic exhibition of hatred, Nazi troops smashed the windows of Jewish merchants and burned *synagogues*, Jewish houses of worship. That night came to be called *Kristallnacht*, meaning "night of glass."

After that, Jews could no longer pretend that they were safe in Germany.

In what they called the "final solution," the Nazis began to imprison, and finally to kill, Jews and everyone else who didn't fit their description of Aryan. This included the Romanies, or gypsies; Communists; the mentally ill; and the physically or mentally handicapped. The entire program of killing people, especially Jews, has come to be called the *Holocaust*, meaning "burned whole." Perhaps as many as 11 million people died in Nazi concentration camps.

A family arrives at a concentration camp.

Scientists Leave Germany

Throughout the nineteenth and twentieth centuries, Germany played an important role in the acquisition of scientific knowledge. Many of the country's scientists were Jews. One of the most famous was the physicist Albert Einstein, who was born in Ulm and grew up in Munich and Milan, Italy. By the time of Hitler's ascent to power, Einstein was fifty-four years old. He had been working on his famous theories, or ideas, of physics for many years. In 1934, the Nazis broke into his home and took all his property. Fortunately, he was working in the United States at the time, and he remained there until his death in 1955. Other physicists working on similar ideas to do with nuclear energy were not so lucky and had to escape however they could.

Most of these physicists later took part in the development of the atomic bomb, two of which were dropped on Japan by the United States in 1945 to end the war. Ironically, Hitler's own scientists had been trying to achieve the same kind of bomb but did not succeed in time.

These camps, where people were imprisoned and worked to death or efficiently murdered, were built throughout Germany, Poland, Czechoslovakia, and other countries that Germany conquered. Anne Frank, the teenage Jewish girl from the Netherlands whose diary was found after the war, died at Bergen-Belsen, near Hanover.

While many teenagers, like Frank, were dying, other German youth were being incorporated into the programs of the Nazi Party. Just when adolescents often feel the most "in between"—neither child nor adult—the party gave boys and girls a feeling of importance by making them a part of the political life of Germany. Hating Jews and other people who were different was just one thing they

Adolf Hitler greets a young Nazi.

learned in their youth organizations. When the war actually started, many young people were already acting like soldiers.

World War II

Hitler and his followers prepared for war. They claimed that Germany needed room to expand, or *Lebensraum* ("living room"), and they planned to create a new empire that would stretch across the whole of Europe.

They started by claiming Austria. Many Austrians welcomed the Germans. Hitler then claimed a German-speaking area of the region of Czechoslovakia called the Sudetenland. Other countries objected to these moves, but no one did anything about them. When Poland appeared to be next, Britain and France promised the Polish people that they would be protected. However, Hitler took everyone by surprise. On September 1, 1939, German troops invaded Poland. War was declared on Germany by Britain and France in support of Poland.

Hitler had prepared his army, navy, and air force well. They took over most of Europe in the coming months. Italy fought on the side of Germany. Eventually, Germany made agreements with Japan, which was aggressively expanding in Asia in

Germany in World War II, 1939–1945

Occupied by Germany
Axis (German) ally
Allied power
Neutral power

much the same way—conquering part of the mainland and killing many people in the process.

Hitler assumed that once he had France he would be able to cross the English Channel and invade Britain. Time after time, though, the German air force was defeated by British combat pilots in the Battle of Britain. Finally Hitler gave up his invasion plans, but for six years of war, England was repeatedly bombed.

A London street after a German bombing

The United States stayed out of the war until December 7, 1941, when Japan bombed the U.S. naval base at Pearl Harbor in Hawaii. Then the United States declared war on both Japan and Germany. Germany, in turn, declared war on the United States.

Hitler's forces turned toward the Soviet Union. In an almost 900-day siege of the city of Leningrad, almost a million people died as they were starved to death. Eventually, perhaps as many as 20 million people died in Russia.

The deadly fingers of war reached throughout the entire world—to Africa, South America, islands in the South Pacific, everywhere. Those fingers kept their grasp on people's lives until 1945.

On June 6, 1944, the military forces of Great Britain, the United States, Canada, Australia, New Zealand, and the other countries that made up the Allies, finally invaded the continent at Normandy, in France, to take the war into Hitler's own lands. It took ten months, but in May 1945, the Germans finally surrendered.

After the war ended, German chancellor Willy Brandt described Germany as "craters, caves, mountains of rubble, debris-covered fields, ruins that hardly allowed one to imagine that they had once been houses . . . no fuel, no light, every little garden a graveyard, and, above all, like an immovable cloud, the stink of putrefaction. In this no man's land lived human beings. Their life was a daily struggle for a handful of potatoes, a loaf of bread, a few lumps of coal."

What to Do with Germany?

During the war, the Allied powers of Britain, the Soviet Union, and the United States agreed that when the war ended, they would divide Germany into zones and occupy them. In this way, they would guarantee that the Germans would never again rise to attack other European nations.

At a meeting called the Yalta Conference, in February 1945, it was decided that France would be given a fourth zone. Germany east of the Oder River would be given to Poland. Berlin, even though it was in the Soviet-occupied area, would be divided among the Allies. The area controlled by the Soviet Union came to be called East Germany, and the larger area controlled by the other Allies formed one nation called West Germany.

The Allies stopped the Nazis by working together, but they were divided on how Germany should be treated. The Soviets wanted it smashed, never able to rebuild, and they wanted Germany to pay large sums of money, called *reparations*, for the damage it caused.

Britain and the United States, however, saw that Germany's economic recovery was important for the recovery of the whole continent. Germany could not recover if it were forced to pay huge reparations.

Starvation remained a way of life and death for many Germans during the next year. Things began to change in 1947 when the new U.S. secretary of state, General George C. Marshall, announced a European recovery program called the Marshall Plan. It called for European nations to decide for themselves what was needed for recovery—all to be paid for by the United States.

Occupied and Divided Germany, 1945–1990

Occupied, 1945–1949	Divided, 1949–1990
American zone	West Germany
British zone	East Germany
French zone	
Russian zone	

The Cold War

World War II was over, but the world would continue to be divided into two parts for several decades—the communist world under the control of the Soviet Union, led by Joseph Stalin, and the noncommunist world dominated by the United States. These two worlds met in the divided German city of Berlin.

The British leader Winston Churchill first used the term *Iron Curtain* in a 1946 speech in Missouri. It came to symbolize the division between those two worlds and to represent the cold war. The cold war was the continuing political struggle between the Soviet, or communist, group of nations, and the Western, capitalist group, led by the United States. For forty years, the two side-by-side German nations—democratic West Germany and communist East Germany—reflected the larger international struggle.

The Berlin Airlift

In the original postwar plans for Germany, the Soviet Union had agreed that the other Allies would always have access to its part of Berlin. However, in 1948, the Soviets tried to get the Western nations out of Berlin by cutting off land, water, and rail access from the west. That left only the air.

The Berlin Airlift was a huge, organized flight program that carried food into the western sectors of Berlin. More than 10,000 tons of food and fuel were needed every day to keep the people in the city alive. Pilots from around the world volunteered to make the dangerous flight into the cut-off city. Flights were run for eleven months before the Soviets gave in and again allowed land access to the city.

In 1948, a council met to create a West German federal government, with states having a great deal of self-government but only a fairly weak central government. Thus the Federal Republic of Germany was created. The Constitution (called the Basic Law) was approved on May 8, 1949.

To the east, the German Democratic Republic, or GDR, officially came into being on October 7, 1949. The GDR covered about one-fifth of the territory that Germany had encompassed before the war. Most natural resources, especially the coal fields and ocean ports, went to the West. Thus, when the Soviets removed everything of value as reparations, East Germany was left with virtually nothing on which to build.

On June 17, 1953, workers in East Germany attempted to revolt against Soviet control. The Soviet Army stopped the rebellion and clamped its fist more tightly on the East Germans.

The Socialist Unity Party under Walter Ulbricht became the major political party of the GDR. He was a German Communist in the 1930s but had fled to the Soviet Union in 1933 when Hitler outlawed all political parties except the Nazi Party.

Under Soviet guidance, Ulbricht's government came to control the East German economy along the same socialist (government owned) principles followed by the Soviet Union. Very quickly, the Soviet Union became the main market for all GDR products. The development of industry took place at the cost of consumer products.

Residents of East Berlin begin a quick escape to the West through their apartment window.

Many East Germans began to leave the country for West Germany, looking for a better life. Most of those who left were young people and people with skills, leaving the GDR with an even more desperate industrial base. The easiest place to leave from was Berlin. The East German government decided to stop people from leaving.

Virtually overnight, on August 13, 1961, the government cut the subway lines, placed barriers across roads, and erected barbed wire fences across Berlin. That barbed wire wall was soon replaced by a solid brick wall. The Berlin Wall was up, and it would remain up for almost thirty years.

A West Berlin guard stands in front of construction as the Berlin Wall is built.

Change Is Coming

For decades it seemed that nothing would change. The cold war would go on between the United States and the Soviet Union. Germany would remain two countries.

Then, in 1985, Mikhail Gorbachev, the general secretary of the Soviet Union, quietly began some political, economic, and social reforms indicating that the government might be loosening its grip. People in East Germany who had kept quiet began to speak up, calling for their own reforms in government.

Demands for reform were made throughout the Communist countries. Hungary, which had been suffering economically for a long time, realized that perhaps the answer to its problems lay in more communication with the West. In September 1989, Hungary took down the barriers between it and Austria. The first breach had been made in the Iron Curtain.

Many East Germans began applying for travel visas to Hungary for holidays. From Hungary, they headed for West Germany. The GDR government tried to stop the flow of people, but it was too late. Those East Germans who had stayed home saw others leaving and began to protest in the streets.

In the city of Leipzig, residents had often gathered at Saint Nicolas Church on Mondays to pray in silent protest at conditions in the once well-to-do city. In September 1989, thousands joined the prayer group and then led a demonstration through the city. Monday after Monday, the protesting group grew larger and more vocal. On November 4, the still-quiet Monday Demonstration had grown to half a million people. On that day a million East Berliners also protested.

A West Berliner swings a sledgehammer trying to destroy the Berlin Wall.

In response to what is called the Peaceful Revolution, the GDR government as a whole resigned on November 7, 1989. Two days later, East German leaders announced they would no longer prevent their citizens from crossing into West Germany. So the Berlin Wall "fell." Enthusiastic demonstrators tore down the actual wall.

Millions of East Germans poured into West Berlin. Most of them soon returned home, glad to have taken a look at the other part of the city for the first time in decades.

Not everyone was happy about the fall of the Berlin Wall and the probable reunification of the two parts of Germany. Unemployment was high, especially in such places as Hamburg and Bremen. West German workers were afraid that East Germans would come and take available jobs at lower wages.

Moves began immediately to reunite the two Germanies. It was not going to be easy. Clearly, East Germany was far behind West Germany in housing and modern industry. Reunification was going to cost a great deal because East Germany had to be brought up to date as quickly as possible.

The New Germany

The Federal Republic of Germany and the German Democratic Republic officially reunited as the Federal Republic of Germany on October 3, 1990. The following March 15, the powers that had occupied Germany for so long—the United States, the United Kingdom (Great Britain), France, and the Soviet Union—gave up all rights to territory or control in Germany. In effect, World War II in Europe was finally over, more than fifty years after it began.

The Federal Republic is now completely intertwined in European and world affairs in a way that it never was in earlier decades. In March 1992, Germany signed the Maastricht Treaty, named after a town in the Netherlands where a summit conference was held. It established the European Union (EU) out of the older European Economic Community, which West Germany had belonged to since its founding. The treaty also created a new currency called the euro. Most EU countries are giving up their old currencies for the new, shared one. People in Germany started using the new coins and bills on January 1, 2002.

Germany was one of the founders of the European Union and is at its heart. Germans, who were once citizens of many small German-speaking states, have entered a new era as citizens of Europe.

The Federal Republic and Berlin

THE FEDERAL REPUBLIC OF GERMANY, OR *BUNDESREPUBLIK* *Deutschland*, is a democratic republic. Its leaders are voted into their jobs by the people, and it has no monarch. It is "federal" because the national government gains its powers from the agreement of the states—called *Länder* (the singular is *Land*)— that make it up. They are a federation.

Opposite: **The Reichstag**

The German Constitution is called the Basic Law. It has been in effect in the Federal Republic since May 23, 1949, and in united Germany since October 3, 1990.

The Federal Government

The federal government of Germany is called the *Bund*. It controls all facets of life that affect all the Länder, such as foreign affairs, defense, currency, taxation, and communications.

Germany's Flag

The flag of the Federal Republic consists of three equal horizontal bands of black, red, and gold. Black is at the top. This flag was designed for use by the short-lived federation of 1848. It was used again by the Weimar Republic and now has been used since 1949.

The individual Länder control education, culture, radio and television, and the environment in their own regions.

The head of the executive branch of government is the chief of state, or president. He or she is elected for a five-year term by a meeting that includes all the members of the Federal Assembly, plus an equal number of delegates elected by the parliaments of the various Länder. The president may be re-elected for one additional five-year term. Most presidential duties are ceremonial in nature, with the president representing the nation.

The head of government is the chancellor, who, like a prime minister, is elected by the Federal Assembly, though only for a four-year term. However, he or she may be re-elected an unlimited number of times. The ministers (cabinet officers) who run the various departments are chosen, or recommended, by the chancellor but must be officially appointed by the president. The chancellor cannot be dismissed during a regular term except by a major decision of the legislature.

German chancellor Gerhard Schroeder

There have been seven chancellors since World War II. Three of them served for long periods: Konrad Adenauer (1949–1963), Helmut Schmidt (1974–1982), and Helmut Kohl (1982–1998). Gerhard Schroeder was elected chancellor in 1998.

The legislative branch, or parliament, consists of two houses. The lower house is the Federal Assembly, or *Bundestag*. The upper house is the Federal Council, or *Bundesrat*.

The Bundestag usually has 669 seats (this number can vary) elected for four years by popular vote. However, a party must win 5 percent of the national vote to be represented in the assembly. In 1998, 31 percent of the members of the Bundestag were women, and the president was a woman, Rita Suessmuth.

The Bundesrat has sixty-nine seats chosen by the Länder governments. Each state has three to six votes, depending on population. The individuals holding these votes represent the political composition of the state, and they must vote together on an issue so that they are actually representing their Land

The Reichstag

The parliament of the German Empire was founded in 1871. Its members decided to build themselves a wonderful legislative building. Called the Reichstag, it was topped by one of the most beautiful domes ever built.

The Reichstag burned in 1933, an event that Adolf Hitler used as an excuse to eliminate the rights of individuals in Germany. The remains of the elegant building were left in the heart of Berlin. On April 30, 1945, the Red Army of the Soviet Union declared their conquest of Berlin by hoisting a Soviet flag over the Reichstag.

In the 1960s, the West German government had part of the building restored, but not to its former glory. That didn't happen until the 1990s, when it was decided to make Berlin the capital once more. On April 19, 1999, the German parliament held its first session in the restored Reichstag.

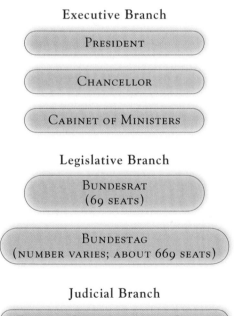

NATIONAL GOVERNMENT OF GERMANY

Executive Branch

PRESIDENT

CHANCELLOR

CABINET OF MINISTERS

Legislative Branch

BUNDESRAT
(69 SEATS)

BUNDESTAG
(NUMBER VARIES; ABOUT 669 SEATS)

Judicial Branch

FEDERAL CONSTITUTIONAL COURT

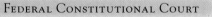

instead of themselves. Each year, a new president of the Bundesrat is chosen, with the position being held by a different state each time.

All citizens are eligible to vote at age eighteen. Women have voted since 1919.

The Communist Party that ruled East Germany for four decades is now called the Party of Democratic Socialists. In 1998, it won seats in the Bundestag for the first time.

The judicial, or court, branch of government consists of the Federal Constitutional Court. Half the judges are appointed by the Bundestag, and half by the Bundesrat. Most court activity is the responsibility of the various states. The federal court becomes involved only when an issue involves more than one state or affects the entire country. Both federal and state judges are appointed to their positions.

A federal judge prepares for the opening session of court.

Helping the Citizens

Germany's Social Security Code guarantees social services to the citizens. The largest part of the nation's budget covers these services. These include old-age pensions, health and accident insurance, family support, unemployment insurance, and free university education. The poor get help paying rent and basic welfare.

All these services come from taxes, which means that individual Germans and companies pay very high taxes. These are both direct income taxes and indirect taxes on purchases, called a value-added tax. In 2001, the government was beginning to show Germans that they would have to stop expecting to receive care permanently.

The International Scene

After the war, European nations began a move to create a "super government" that would help each nation recover from

The National Anthem

The words to Germany's national anthem come from the third verse of *Deutschlandlied*, a poem by August Heinrich Hoffman von Fallersleben, written in 1841. It is set to music from Josef Haydn's "Emperor" Quartet.

Unity and Right and Freedom
For the German fatherland,
Let us all pursue this purpose,
Fraternally with heart and hand.
Unity and Right and Freedom
Are the pledge of happiness.
Flourish in this blessing's glory,
Flourish, German fatherland

German troops participating in the International Security Assistance Force in Kabul, Afghanistan, 2002.

the war and improve economically. West Germany was one of the founders of this super government, called the European Economic Community. Popularly called the Common Market, it was founded in 1957 with six nations, including West Germany, signing the Treaties of Rome that organized it. By working together as one economic unit on the world market, they could compete with the United States and other economically powerful nations. Now called the European Union (EU), it has most European nations among its members.

Germany has long been known for its powerful military, based especially on Prussia's earlier dominance in Europe. Other European nations were afraid to let Germany have an army again after it drove the world into two massive wars.

Today's military, called the *Bundeswehr*, is comparatively small. The Allies gave West Germany permission to form a purely defensive force in 1955. It grew until the Berlin Wall fell. At that time, the militaries of East and West Germany were unified, but since then the number of people and weapons has shrunk. German troops participate in many activities of the North Atlantic Treaty Organization, such as serving in the countries that once formed Yugoslavia, which are fighting among themselves.

German Länder

The Federal Republic of Germany is made up of sixteen Länder, or states. Three of them are actually cities and their metropolitan areas. These are Berlin, Bremen, and Hamburg.

The Länder as they are defined today have little to do with the historic regions occupied by the various countries of German history. They were decided as a result of agreements among the Allied powers after World War II.

Like U.S. states, Länder have considerable power to control action within their borders. Each state has a legislature, or *Landtag*, with a prime minister and cabinet to deal with the state's affairs. The Landtags can pass their own laws pertaining to culture, security within their borders, and education.

Sixteen States

1 Baden-Württemberg	
2 Bavaria	
5 Bremen	
6 Hamburg	
7 Hesse	
8 Lower Saxony	
10 North Rhine-Westphalia	
11 Rhineland-Palatinate	
12 Saarland	
15 Schleswig-Holstein	

Formerly East Germany

3 Berlin
4 Brandenburg
9 Mecklenburg-West Pomerania
13 Saxony
14 Saxony-Anhalt
16 Thuringia

Changing Capitals

When the German Empire was formed in 1871, Berlin was made the capital of the new nation. It remained so until 1949, when the East Germans, controlled by the Soviet Union, made their sector of Berlin, East Berlin, into their capital.

Although the Allies controlled a large portion of Berlin, the West Germans were unable to make West Berlin their capital. At first this was because it was so difficult to reach it through East Germany. After 1971, although, an agreement among the occupying powers declared that West Berlin was not part of West Germany, although the West Germans regarded West Berlin as one of their states. They chose the small university town of Bonn as their capital.

In choosing a capital after unification in 1990, two ideas came into play. Bonn, as capital of the Federal Republic, represented to the people the stability and growth of European partnerships of the past forty-five years. Berlin, on the other hand, was seen by some to represent Germany's troubled and violent past. However, placing the capital in Berlin served to reunite the two Germanies as nothing else could. In the Bundestag, the vote was very close—338 to 320 in favor of Berlin.

As the capital, Bonn had been changed from a small university town, most famous for its connection to the composer Ludwig van Beethoven to a booming city. When the capital was moved to Berlin, at least eight major ministries were kept in Bonn. Plans are being made to make Bonn the focus of technological advances in Germany.

The Brandenburg Gate

Berlin was a walled city in the 1700s. At that time its main street was Unter den Linden, which was originally just a path from the palace marked by linden trees. A gate was built that would allow traffic to flow through the wall and onto Unter den Linden. This became the famed Brandenburg Gate, which is topped by a statue of the Goddess of Victory driving four horses. For the next 200 years, the gate and area around it became the focus of celebrations and victory marches.

The gate was closed when the Berlin Wall was erected. It remained closed for almost thirty years.

It was reopened on December 22, 1989. The Brandenburg Gate has now become the symbol of reunification.

Checkpoint Charlie

The Berlin Wall sealed East Germans into their small section of Berlin. Soon after it went up, the Soviets tried to prevent the Western powers from entering East Germany through Berlin. In October 1961, U.S. and Soviet tanks faced each other, and a new war seemed about to begin. However, after two days, the Soviets backed down and agreed to abide by the earlier agreement that the other Allies would have access to Berlin.

The two sides built an elaborate gate, Checkpoint C, at Friedrichstrasse, called Checkpoint Charlie, (Checkpoints A and B were on the freeway leading to Berlin). It was at this narrow site that the tanks faced each other.

Until the Berlin Wall came down, Checkpoint Charlie was the only place where foreign visitors could pass into East Berlin. The Western powers had a gate, and on the other side the Soviets had their gate. In between was an open space called "no man's land." Many buildings around the checkpoint were demolished, leaving an empty strip through the heart of Berlin. Several times, East Germans tried to escape through Checkpoint Charlie and were shot down by East German border guards.

Checkpoint Charlie was dismantled after reunification, and the Allied guardhouses went to a museum. A replica of the American guardhouse was constructed on its original site in 2000. The East German watchtower is being replaced by office buildings and shops.

Berlin: Did You Know This?

Berlin was probably founded near the beginning of the thirteenth century, on the Spree River. Its name first appears in records in 1244. It remained fairly small until Frederick William, called the Great Elector of Brandenburg, started building a canal that connected Berlin to the shipping ports in the north.

Much of the old beauty of Berlin comes from the graceful buildings erected under the Prussians. There are few skyscrapers because the city is built on a huge underground river, called an aquifer. That is wonderful for the city's water supplies but bad for building huge, heavy buildings. Consequently, Berlin is spread out over a larger area than most old cities. It covers 341 square miles (883 sq km).

People live in friendly neighborhoods that grew out of the many towns and communities that were long ago incorporated into Greater Berlin. Each neighborhood still has its original town hall. The huge Tiergarten and many other parks and gardens keep the city green.

Almost 60 percent of the city of Berlin was heavily bombed by the end of World War II. Seventy percent

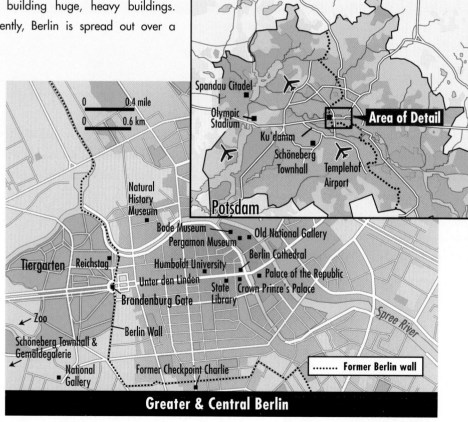

of the old inner city was destroyed. After the war, West Berlin was cleaned up at incredible speed and began to thrive again. East Berlin was another matter. Author Robert Brustein described East Berlin in 1964 as "less a city than a perpetuated heap of rubble intended to remind people of the war."

The Berlin Wall meandered 96 miles (154 km) through the vast city. On both sides of the wall, the ground was left bare. Land mines were planted on the eastern side of the wall to prevent people from trying to climb over it. When the wall came down, a barren strip was left through the city. This strip is being filled with new buildings, gardens, and homes.

Berlin is emerging as the focus of the varied media businesses of Europe—publishing, Internet, movies, advertising, and theater. In 2001, two huge music publishing and recording companies—Universal Music and Sony—moved to Berlin. The city has also become a major convention site because so many people from all over the world want to see for themselves the miracle of Berlin's recovery.

In 2001, the metropolitan area called Greater Berlin was reorganized into twelve districts. There are now more than 3 million people in Greater Berlin. This figure is on its way back to the 4.5 million that lived there before World War II.

Population (2001 est.): 3,458,763

Year founded: 1230–1240

Altitude: 180 feet (55 m) above sea level

Average daily temperature: January, 31°F (–1°C); July, 66°F (19°C)

Average annual rainfall: 23 inches (58 cm)

The German Miracle

GERMANY IS THE WORLD'S THIRD MOST POWERFUL ECONomy. Only the United States and Japan produce and spend more. This is truly amazing because when World War II ended, Germany was a nation in ruins, its dreams destroyed; its infrastructure of streets, bridges, and utilities broken; its industrial base crushed. Even a large chunk of the nation itself was gone, given to Poland.

The Allied nations knew that their failure to help Germany after World War I had played an important part in bringing on World War II. They were determined not to repeat that mistake. The Marshall Plan, backed by the United States, was a commitment to help Germany rebuild, both physically and economically. The speed with which this rebuilding took place has been called the German miracle.

Germany is now primarily a service economy. Almost two-thirds of the employed people work in businesses that directly help people rather than manufacture things. Manufacturing, or the industrial sector, employs one-third, while agriculture employs fewer than 3 percent of the people.

Opposite: **Manufacturing contributes to one-third of the economy in Germany.**

Since World War II, the German economy rose, creating an economically powerful country.

System of Weights and Measures

The metric system is Germany's system of weights and measures. Lengths are expressed in meters; weight, in grams; and liquid measures, in liters.

Forty-Five Years of GDR Economy

Due to the way Germany was partitioned, East Germany had a smaller population and fewer resources than West Germany. In addition, the Soviet Union took most of East Germany's money as reparations for war damage.

Given those conditions, it's amazing that the nation survived as well as it did. It didn't just survive—it became an important industrial economy, providing goods on the global market. It became the wealthiest country in eastern Europe on a per person (per capita) basis. Not even the Soviet Union was as well-off.

However, this prosperity came at the expense of many other things. There were few consumer goods. Factory equipment deteriorated and was not replaced. Housing was inadequate. The water, air, and land were severely polluted. When the Berlin Wall came down, the country was almost bankrupt from having to import almost everything it needed.

When the Wall Came Down

The new, reunified Germany became responsible for fixing the terrible economic conditions in what had been the GDR. It was not easy, and conditions did not improve instantly. The market with the Soviet Union disappeared almost overnight. Also, factories were sadly out of date and harmed the environment. A large number of factories were closed, government jobs disappeared, and eastern German unemployment rose.

The Euro

In 1948, a new currency was established in West Germany. It was the *Deutschmark* (DM), which replaced the old *Reichsmark*. The DM was made up of 100 *Pfennig* (the word from which our "penny" comes). The DM was one of the most stable currencies in Europe for decades.

The DM has now disappeared into the euro system of the European Union (EU). The EU hopes that trade with other parts of the world will improve when it can all be done in only one currency instead of eight or ten different ones.

Banks introduced the new currency at the beginning of 1999. At the beginning of 2002, Germany became the first nation to fully change over to the euro. Within a very short time, 71,500 tons of new euro coins and 2.5 billion new bills went into circulation, and all the old currency was removed.

The labor unions of the former West Germany didn't want the easterners taking jobs at lower wages. They insisted that they had to earn as much as workers in the West. Few workers from eastern Germany could find jobs at such pay scales.

The East German industrial complex was put in the hands of an agency called the THA (for *Treuhandanstalt*). It decided which factories could be preserved and tried to find buyers for them. Those factories that made useful, good-quality products for which there was a market were generally bought by Western industrialists and kept open. Within the first four years, the THA sold more than 14,500 companies to investors in the United Kingdom, Switzerland, and France.

Many West Germans resented the amount of money the government invested in the East German Länder. The money came out of their own pockets because they had to pay higher income taxes to support the transformation of eastern Germany.

A worker opens a sluice gate in a steel mill.

By the year 2023, Germany will no longer operate nuclear power plants.

The Ruhr Valley has some of the richest coal fields and iron ore deposits in Europe. Consequently, it has long been a center of iron and steel production. The largest deposits of iron ore are in Lower Saxony, near the Harz Mountains. The country once had a fair amount of copper and silver, but they are mostly gone.

Most of the coal in the Ruhr Valley is anthracite, or hard coal. Hard coal burns with a high heat and little pollution. About 26 percent of Germany's energy comes from anthracite. Unfortunately, a larger amount—31 percent—comes from burning soft coal, or lignite, which is all that eastern Germany has available. Soft coal burns inefficiently and pollutes the atmosphere in many ways.

About 28 percent of Germany's electric power comes from nuclear power plants. The GDR's nuclear power plants were badly built. They have all been shut down. In 2001, the government signed a plan to shut down all of Germany's nineteen remaining nuclear power plants within twenty-one years.

Most of the petroleum Germany uses must be imported, which makes it expensive. Natural gas, which is more readily available, supplies about 21 percent of the country's needs. It is expected that natural gas usage will increase as nuclear power plants are eliminated. Wind power is also being developed.

Agriculture

When the Soviets took control of the eastern zone, they put all farms of more than 250 acres (101 hectares), as well as all land that belonged to former Nazis, under government control. This land was given to laborers according to communist principles of equal ownership. Soon, though, even the largest of those farms were also broken up, so that farming became inefficient.

In order to function, the various small farms in a region had to organize themselves into groups called collectives. Each collective owned the machinery used in plowing and harvesting, and it determined what each farmer could plant. Realizing that they could no longer farm as they wished, many farmers tried to leave for the West.

What Germany Grows, Makes, and Mines

Agriculture

Fodder	56,526,000 metric tons
Sugar beets	27,568,800 metric tons
Wheat	19,615,300 metric tons
Barley	13,301,000 metric tons

Manufacturing

Cement	38,099,000 metric tons
Rolled steel	16,881,000 metric tons
Household plastics	12,665,000 metric tons

Mining

Lignite (soft coal)	166,277,000 metric tons
Anthracite (hard coal)	39,523,170 metric tons
Salt	8,405,000 metric tons

Vineyard workers pick grapes above the Mosel River.

The Federal Republic was once a nation of small farms. In recent years, however, many of these farms have merged into big agricultural industries. They respond to the instructions of the European Union. Today, agriculture is about 3 percent of the German economy. The major crops are grains, fruit, sugar beets, cabbage, potatoes, and flowers.

The slopes of the valleys along the Rhine and Mosel Rivers have long been important regions for growing grapes. The grapes are used to make well-known white wines.

The People's Car—Volkswagen

The Volkswagen (VW) was designed in 1934 by Ferdinand Porsche as an inexpensive car meant for "the people." In 1938, Adolf Hitler officially opened the factory where they would be built. He called the car the "Strength through Joy" wagon. Then the factory turned to war machinery, and the People's Car was not built on a mass scale until after the war, when the British found the factory in their sector. Several kinds of cars were assembled, but not until 1949 was the design that came to be called the Beetle put into production. By 1972, the Volkswagen Beetle had become the most popular car ever built, surpassing the famed old Model T Ford.

Carmakers and Other Industry

Among the most important industrial firms in the world are some that existed before World War II but that became internationally important after the war. Daimler-Benz and Volkswagen, for example, are automobile manufacturers. Daimler-Benz is now Daimler-Chrysler since merging with Chrysler, which was the third-largest U.S. carmaker. It still makes the luxurious Mercedes-Benz cars. The BMW (for Bavarian Motor Works), headquartered in Munich, is also popular the world over. The BMW Museum is there. Audi also opened an automobile museum, called Museum Mobile, in Ingolstadt in 2000. Audi has been in the automobile business since 1909.

A Trabant owner services his vehicle, keeping it in good running condition.

Those East Germans who could afford cars but who were not part of the political elite usually drove East German–made cars call Trabants, which were manufactured in Zwickau. These two-cylinder-engine cars were popularly called "little stinkers." In recent years, owners of the few remaining Trabants have become proud of them.

The 150-year-old electrical engineering and electronics firm of Siemens, headquartered in Munich, provides materials for use around the world. It makes everything from computer-controlled railroads to cordless phones. An international giant in communications, Deutsch Telekom, is headquartered in Bonn.

Germany was one of the most important nations in the world in the early days of the chemical industry. The famed firm of Bayer was founded at Elberfeld in 1863 as a dye company. In 1897, one of its employees, Dr. Felix Hoffman, discovered the pain-relieving property of a chemical called acetylsalicylic acid, better known today as aspirin. Like Bayer, the firm of BASF started in 1865 in Ludwigshafen as a dye-maker. Today, it makes everything from plastics to compact disks to telephone wire to chemicals that make cattle grow faster.

High-speed trains are a popular means of travel in Germany.

Transportation

Germany has had railroads since 1838, when the first one was built between Berlin and Potsdam. Today, Germany is crisscrossed by a number of efficient, high-speed railways, especially the ICE (InterCity Express) trains. A train route from Berlin to Hanover was opened in 1998, after years of little train traffic through eastern Germany.

Considerable work has been applied to the Transrapid between Berlin and Hamburg. Called maglev, for "magnetic levitation," it is planned as a high-speed train that is raised off its track by a powerful magnetic force. However, it may be too expensive to build.

The maglev at a station along a test route in Elmsland, Germany

Throughout the years of separation, air traffic in and out of Berlin was under the Allied military control. As soon as reunification occurred, the German airline Lufthansa began once again flying into Berlin.

The biggest airport in Germany is at Frankfurt, because that's where U.S. military troops took off and landed for many years. Berlin has three airports: Tegel, which is virtually in the city; Schönefeld, 11 miles (18 km) out of the city in what was the East; and the historic Templehof, which was used for the Berlin Airlift and is now flown into and out of by most European carriers.

Tourism

In 2000, more than 16 million visitors came to see the sights of Germany. Almost every town has an old church, town

Tourists enjoying a day of sightseeing in Brandenburg

center, or castle that has survived time and wars and has been cleaned up for visitors to enjoy. Visitors to West Germany had known about the joys of the quaint towns for a long time, but East Germany was a long way from being an attractive place to visit when the wall came down.

Concerted efforts were made to modernize many towns that had been allowed to deteriorate during the GDR years. Stores and offices were updated and rebuilt. Housing was quickly improved. Wherever possible, the historic town centers have been preserved. The only way this could be done in many towns was by not allowing cars into historic areas.

In 2001, it was trendy for Germans from the western part of the country to buy things that were made in eastern Germany. These attractive items make Westerners realize that perhaps life wasn't so hard and colorless in the east as they had been led to believe.

The Cuckoo Clock

The Black Forest region is known the world over for its hand-carved cuckoo clocks. It's said that the first one was produced in the village of Schönwald near Triberg in the 1700s. The ornate hand-carved cabinets are made of many different woods, but the real skill is in making a tiny bird that can produce sounds at two pitches, making the familiar *cu-koo*. Bellows of two sizes release air along with different sounds when the bird pops out of a door on the hour.

Who Is a German?

T HROUGHOUT HISTORY, GERMANY HAS BEEN — AT THE SAME time—many small nations spread through a vast region of eastern Europe, and one land held together by related cultures. One of the most common questions for many years has been, "Who is a German?"

Perhaps it is someone who speaks the German language and shares the culture of that language. If so, Germans live in a much greater territory than that occupied today by Germany. Perhaps it is a citizen of today's Germany. If so, many people who have kept their native language cannot call themselves Germans.

Today, the question is still being asked because Germany has become a place for people to seek asylum. They are looking for protection and safety from persecution in other countries.

Opposite: **A boy in traditional lederhosen**

Who Lives in Germany? (2001 est.)

German	91.5%
Turkish	2.4%
Other (includes Danish, Serbo-Croatian, Italian, Russian, Greek, Polish, Spanish)	6.1%

Germany is one of the most heavily populated countries in Europe.

The Numbers

Germany has a population of about 83 million. After the Russian Federation, Germany has more people than any other country in Europe. However, it is smaller in area than France, which has only about 59 million people.

Germany is one of the most densely populated countries in Europe, averaging 596 people per square mile (230 per sq km). Only Belgium, the Netherlands, and the

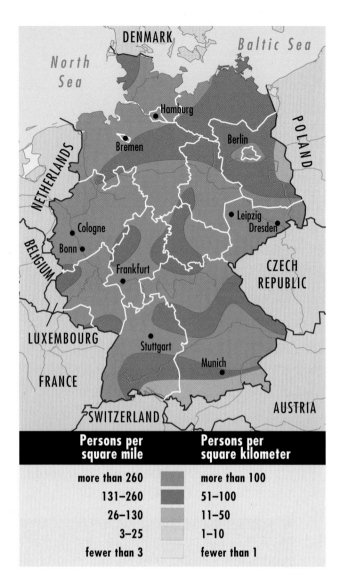

Persons per square mile / Persons per square kilometer

Persons per square mile		Persons per square kilometer
more than 260		more than 100
131–260		51–100
26–130		11–50
3–25		1–10
fewer than 3		fewer than 1

United Kingdom have higher population densities. The two densest areas are Berlin, where about 3.4 million people live, and the Rhine-Ruhr industrial area. This region is so tightly packed that it has a population density of 3,107 per square mile (1,200 per sq km).

In 1939, the Länder that became East Germany were occupied by 16.7 million people. Throughout World War II, the number increased by almost 2 million as people fled from the war-torn areas farther east. When the two parts of Germany were separated, East Germany was left with about one-fifth of the population of West Germany. Between 1950 and 1990, West Germany's population rose from 50.8 million to 61.5 million.

Where and How They Live

In the areas that made up West Germany, the largest proportion of people live in cities and towns. In eastern Germany, more people live in rural areas. More than half of all Germans today live in rented apartments. Those who own their own houses or condominiums are primarily in the western portion, though home ownership is increasing in the eastern Länder.

People who live along the onetime border between East and West often benefit from their location. Those in the eastern Länder readily shop and sometimes work in the nearby western towns. Those in the western Länder often take advantage of the less expensive child care found in the towns that were once in East Germany.

Most Germans live in modern apartment buildings.

The Language

Throughout the centuries, many small states developed their own dialects, or varieties, of the German language. They varied in pronunciation, meanings of words, and introduction of new words. German was first given a grammar about A.D. 790, when Charlemagne ordered his scribes to record sagas of the Frankish people. Today, there are still several spoken varieties of German, though television and radio are making them more alike.

Basically, there are two varieties of spoken German—High German and Low German. High German is also called Standard

A group of friends chat at an outdoor café.

German. Used in public communications, it is the spoken form of written German. Written German is very much the same wherever German is used. It stems primarily from the translation of the Bible into written German by Martin Luther.

Written German has a punctuation mark called an umlaut. It consists of two dots over a vowel, usually *a*, *o*, or *u*. People in different regions of Germany pronounce words with an umlaut differently, but basically it raises the sound of the vowel—literally lifts your tongue to the roof of your mouth while your lips make the vowel's shape. You can see sometimes, in German names that have been translated into English, where an umlaut has been eliminated. "Müller," for example, becomes "Mueller." The wind called the Föhn becomes the "Foehn."

In the late 1990s, agreement was reached in making some changes in the German language. The advocates for change wanted, for example, to eliminate some of the uses of the letter ß, which is kind of like a double ss. Also, because

Street and shop signs in written German

descriptive words are often attached to nouns, sometimes words get very long. It was recommended that some of these be broken up into several words. However, there has been little evidence that the public is willing to make these changes.

Low German has been spoken mostly in western Germany where the tribes of Saxons lived. They took it to England, where the English language acquired a rich German base. Today, Low German is similar to Dutch.

Schleswig and Holstein, on the Jutland Peninsula, belonged to Denmark for many centuries. Denmark lost those two territories to the German Confederation in 1866. Many of the people in the former Schleswig still speak Danish as their primary language, though in the former Holstein they are more apt to speak Low German.

The ethnic group called Sorbs, or Wends, has lived for centuries in northeastern Germany. They also have their own language, which is related to Slavic.

Starting in the early 1980s, some public schools offered bilingual, or two-language, education—in German and Turkish, for instance—to help immigrants ease into German society. However, by 2000, many neighborhood schools, especially in Berlin, were mostly Turkish, and the children did not have much opportunity to learn German. Bilingual education has been dropped in most schools, and children are forced to learn German.

Some Common German Terms

Guten Tag.	Hello; good-day.
Auf wiedersehen.	Good-bye.
Bitte	Please
Danke schön.	Thank you.
Ja	Yes
Nein	No
Ich verstehe nicht.	I do not understand.

Much of West Germany's population increase was due to the number of immigrant workers who entered the country and then brought their families. Many of the immigrants were of German ethnic background and thus were automatically citizens under the Basic Law.

Within the first five years after World War II, almost 17 percent of West Germany's population was made up of refugees from the Soviets in the East, especially from East Prussia and the Baltic region. After the Berlin Wall went up, the growth of the West German economy depended on new workers coming from non-German countries, such as Italy, Spain, and Turkey. By contrast, only a few foreign laborers were allowed into the GDR, and most of them were from Vietnam.

This foreign worker from Mongolia shows his permission to work in Germany.

Today, about 7.3 million of the people living in Germany—about 9 percent—are foreigners, meaning that they belong to ethnic groups other than German.

The Basic Law, Germany's constitution, allows anyone to seek asylum in Germany on grounds of political persecution. This was written into the Basic Law after the war as a way of atoning for the earlier years of kicking people out, or even enslaving people who were regarded as non-German.

From 1989 to 1992, however, almost a million people sought asylum in Germany, more than in any other European country. On July 1, 1993, the Basic Law was revised to require that refugees could seek asylum only if they were from countries internationally recognized as persecuting certain members of their citizenry. This reduced the number of asylum-seekers.

It's difficult for people who work hard for a living to accept strangers in their midst when the government seems to give these strangers everything they need. Sometimes groups of young men attack the foreigners. These extremists are often called neo-Nazis (meaning "new Nazis") or skinheads (because of their tendency to shave their heads). Most responsible Germans, though, are determined never to let extremists gain control of Germany again. In 2001, the German government began to encourage neo-Nazis to quit racist organizations by offering them housing and jobs.

Many Germans are trying to keep nationalism—the pride in identifying oneself as German—separate from hatred for people who are not German. This will be one of Germany's tasks for the future.

A small percentage of people living in Germany are originally from other countries.

Population of Major Cities (2000 est.)	
Berlin (2001 est.)	3,458,763
Hamburg	1,707,986
Munich	1,225,809
Cologne	964,346
Frankfurt	647,304

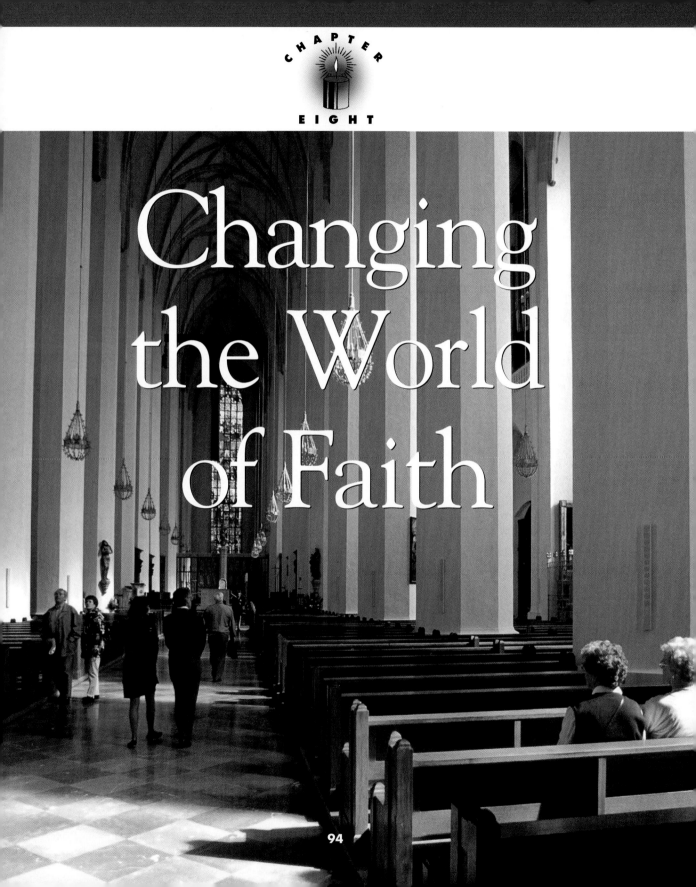

Changing the World of Faith

THE EARLIEST GERMANS BELIEVED IN MANY GODS, AND they told stories about them to explain events in their world. The most powerful god was Wotan, sometimes called Odin. He was the god of both wisdom and war. As the Germanic tribes spread through Scandinavia and Britain, these gods went with them.

Some of the characters and gods reappeared about 1200 in an epic poem called the *Nibelungenlied* (*Song of the Nibelung*). The unknown author collected ballads, lengthy poems, that had long been sung to pass on ancient stories of the people. The *Nibelungenlied* told the absurd, sad, and heroic tales of German gods and goddesses interfering in the life of a dragon-slaying human adventurer named Siegfried, who represents faithfulness. Despite great hardships, he refuses to tell where a great treasure, the Nibelung, has been hidden.

The poem had virtually disappeared through the centuries until it was rediscovered in the mid-1700s. Since then, it has served as the basis for many German tales, musical works, and the like. In the nineteenth century, German composer Richard Wagner created a series of powerful operas based on the *Nibelungenlied*.

The Beginning of Christianity

As in most places, Christianity and *paganism* (the belief in many gods) lived side by side for many years. However,

Opposite: **Christianity was brought to Germany from Rome in the early 700s.**

Christianity began to overtake the old religion in the eighth century, especially under the leadership of a missionary from England. He took the name Boniface, which is probably derived from the Latin for "good faith." He was sent by the pope in Rome in A.D. 719 to preach to the Germans.

Boniface was determined to keep the native people from returning to paganism. In one town, he cut down a tree dedicated to the old god of thunder, Thor, and had it built into a chapel. When Thor didn't strike Boniface down, the tribal people in the surrounding area gave up paganism and became Christians. At a meeting in Holland, Boniface and many other Christians were ambushed and killed by enraged nonbelievers. He was regarded as a martyred saint, Saint Boniface, for dying for his faith.

Not many years later, Charlemagne put Christianity at the center of his Holy Roman Empire. Most Germans did the same, putting the church at the center of their lives.

Crusades and Knights

Starting about 1095, the various Christian countries of Europe were busy arguing among themselves, primarily about territory. The pope in Rome stopped the squabbling by showing them that the Muslims of the Middle East were growing too powerful, that they were destroying some important holy sites.

Suddenly pilgrimages, which are journeys with a religious purpose, became very important to European Christians. When pilgrims to holy places were attacked, European armies set out to avenge and protect them.

Thus began centuries of wars between Christians and Muslims. Many of these wars were kept up for political reasons and had nothing to do with religion. It was important for young knights to prove their courage by going on a holy Crusade.

Many soldiers from Germany went to fight, but it wasn't until 1190 that the religious order of German knights called the Knights of the Teutonic Order was founded. It became an important religious and military army that fought through the coming centuries and played a role in the founding of Prussia. The fighting religious order survived until the early 1800s.

A knight of the Teutonic Order returning from a Crusade.

Great Cathedrals and Charming Churches

One of the glories from the Middle Ages is the great cathedrals built throughout Europe. They are often both massive and delicate, with great towers and carvings of real and imaginary scenes. Germany has a dozen or more cathedrals remaining, but the greatest is at Cologne (pictured), which is one of the largest cathedrals ever built. Its twin spires are 515 feet (157 m) high. The building of the cathedral was started in 1248, but it was not finished until 1880. It was partially bombed in World War II and has been rebuilt.

Other, usually smaller, churches built in the 1700s are in the style called rococo, which comes from a French word meaning "rockwork." These churches have numerous gold curlicues, walls with pictures painted on them, and other whimsical flourishes, with no strong straight lines anywhere.

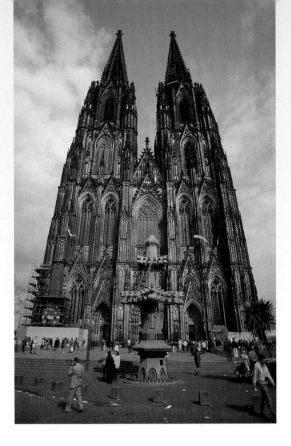

The Reformation

Legend says that on October 31, 1517, a priest named Martin Luther nailed a written-out version of his beliefs (later called the 95 Theses) to the door of the Castle Church at Wittenberg. This has been called the start of the Protestant Reformation.

Luther probably did not actually do that. Instead, he wrote to his superiors, outlining his beliefs. He especially opposed the sale of "indulgences." An indulgence was forgiveness of sin that could be purchased instead of going to confession and asking God's forgiveness. The people who bought indulgences (at different prices depending on the gravity of the offense) figured that they didn't really have to feel remorse and promise not to sin again, as they would if they confessed to a priest. Catholic Church officials liked indulgences because they brought in money to the church.

During the following years, Luther published criticisms of the *papacy* (the establishment of the pope as head of the Catholic Church). He showed that politics and religion were completely intertwined. He wrote a great deal and translated the New Testament of the Bible into German. This was the first time the Bible was available to German people in their own language.

Luther the Reformer

Born in 1483 in Eisleben, the son of a copper worker, Martin Luther attended the University of Erfurt, where he was laughingly called "The Philosopher." In 1505, he entered an Augustinian monastery in Erfurt to become a monk (below). After being ordained as a priest, the intelligent young man was sent to Wittenberg University, where he later became a professor of biblical theology.

When Luther starting complaining about indulgences, he had no intention of starting a revolution in

religion. He was protesting purely against one aspect of the Catholic Church of Rome. However, once he started, he continued to write and speak whenever he could. In January 1521, Pope Leo X excommunicated Luther. That meant that he no longer had the right to participate in the sacraments of the church.

The Diet of the Holy Roman Empire (an assembly of delegates) met at Worms that year and called Luther to appear before them. They were disturbed at the amount of public attention he was getting. The Diet demanded that he recant, or take back, the things he had said against the church.

Luther replied, "I neither can nor will recant anything, for it is neither right nor safe to act against conscience."

In 1525, Luther, no longer officially a Catholic priest, married Katharina von Bora, a former nun. They had seven children. In 1546, Luther went to Eisleben, where he had been born, to settle an argument. While there, he became ill and died at the age of sixty-three.

The Passion Play

The small Alpine town of Oberammergau in Bavaria is known both for its wood carvings and for its long-running passion play. A passion play is a theatrical performance showing the last week of the life of Christ, before he was crucified. In the 1630s, the terrible disease called the plague, or the black death, killed millions of people throughout Europe. When it reached Oberammergau, the villagers promised God that if he would spare the people of the town, they would perform a passion play every ten years forever. No more villagers died, and the play has been performed virtually every ten years ever since.

In the meantime, the Reformation, as a revolt against the traditional Catholic Church, was spreading. In England, King Henry VIII became a Protestant when he broke with Rome over divorcing his wives. French theologian John Calvin took up the Reformation and was persecuted for it. His followers were called Huguenots, and they were thrown out of France. Many went to Germany to live; others went to American colonies. Eventually, Calvin's beliefs led to the formation of the Presbyterian Church.

Jews in Germany

Jews began to settle in Germany in the tenth century. They came primarily from France and Italy. They were never a very large part of the population, but they often stood out because they strongly believed in education. They also kept up various

Jewish men pray inside an East Berlin synagogue.

religious practices that made them seem different. Over many centuries, there grew to be an undercurrent of anti-Jewish, or anti-Semitic, feeling in Germany and many other places.

Throughout much of the nineteenth and early twentieth centuries, the Jews of Germany were restricted in the work they could do. They were allowed into only those professions that the Germans of the upper classes had no interest in, such as business, medicine, and law. The German aristocrats, especially the Prussians, kept the military and the civil service for themselves.

By the 1930s, there were still only about 600,000 Jews in Germany, not more than 1 percent of the population. About one-third of them lived in Berlin.

From his earliest days of writing and speaking, Adolf Hitler insisted that Jews were to blame for Germans' suffering, economically and culturally. When he gained power in 1933, the Nazis sent many Jews into concentration camps for "protective custody." Many Jews who had the funds and realized that the situation was serious fled Germany for other countries. Many intellectuals and scientists came to the United States.

After World War II actually began, some concentration camps were modified to kill the people sent to them instead of just to house them. Among the first to die were Jews. Communists were also sent to the camps and, later, any Protestants and Catholics who had the courage to speak out. After the war, only 1 percent of the German Jews—or 6,000—remained alive. Today, Jews around the world observe Holocaust

Remembrance Day on May 2. The number of Jews in Germany didn't increase until after the Berlin Wall was brought down.

Churches Against Hitler

Pope Pius XI, who died in 1939, protested in writing against Hitler's control of Germany. He insisted that humans were entitled to certain rights and that the Nazis were denying those rights. His successor, Pope Pius XII, also protested, but not enough. When Jews began to be gathered in Rome in 1943 and sent to concentration camps to die, the pope did not protest. There are arguments to this day about whether Pius XII should have tried to interfere.

Most of the churches within Germany were silent about the Nazis, primarily because the government took control of them early on. However, two Lutheran ministers, Martin Niemöller and Dietrich Bonhöfer, openly opposed the political control of the church by the Nazis. Bonhöfer was executed, as were other members of the group the two had formed. Niemöller was imprisoned for seven years.

Today's Churches

Early followers of the Reformation were called Lutherans as an insult by the people who opposed them, but the name gradually caught on among the protesting people, too. Today, the Lutheran Church is international. In the United States, it is the fourth-largest Protestant denomination.

After World War II, most people declared themselves members of one church or another. Lutherans had to pay a tax above their income taxes to support their church, whether they attended services or not. In the 1980s, well over 2 million Germans gave up their membership in Lutheran churches in order to stop paying that tax.

Various other Protestant churches, including Methodists and Baptists, are called free churches because they are free of all ties to the state. They are supported only by the donations made by members.

More than 2 million residents of Germany—almost 2 percent of the people—are Muslims. There has been a *mosque* (a Muslim house of worship) and a center for studying the Koran in Berlin since 1927.

Today, most Muslims are primarily workers and their families who moved from Turkey in the 1950s and 1960s. In the 1990s, though, their number increased with Kurds, Pakistanis, and Iranians seeking asylum. Islamic American soldiers stationed in Germany also brought the Muslim presence to the country. In 2001, work began on a large mosque in the Cologne area, large enough for 1,000 people to worship.

Important Religious Holidays

Good Friday	March or April
Easter	Sunday in March or April
Ascension Thursday	May
Pentecost	Sunday in May or June
Christmas	December 25

Young boys study the Koran at the central mosque in Berlin.

Creators
and Athletes

NO MATTER WHICH PARTICULAR LITTLE COUNTRY THEY lived in over the centuries, the German people have a long history of involvement in the arts. They have been at the center of European culture. Their literature, art, and music continue to be significant today.

Opposite: **Johann Sebastian Bach, one of Germany's premier composers**

The Ornate Baroque

Germany was at the heart of the baroque movement in art, architecture, and music from about 1600 to about 1800.

Baroque art might be defined as exuberant, or lively, after the quite restrained art of earlier years. Some of the more dramatic palaces in Germany are expressions of baroque worldly splendor. The Zwinger Palace (now a major art museum) in Dresden shows baroque style in its architecture. The rococo buildings of later years represent a type of baroque. The fantastic rococo castle of *Sanssouci* ("Without Care," in French) is located at Potsdam.

Johann Sebastian Bach represents the baroque in music, as does George Frideric Handel (composer of *Messiah*), though he spent most of his working years in England. Bach, born in Eisenach in 1685,

Sanssouci Castle is an example of baroque architecture.

was court violinist in Weimar when he wrote many of his works for the organ. He moved to Cöthen, where he wrote many orchestral works, including the great Brandenburg Concertos. On a simpler note were the beautiful pieces of *The Well-Tempered Clavier* (a keyboard instrument). Moving on to Leipzig, Bach composed numerous choral works called cantatas, originally meant for a school choir. His greatest choral work was the *Saint Matthew Passion*. Several of his many children, including Johann Christian and Carl Philip Emmanuel, also became renowned composers.

A century later, composer Ludwig van Beethoven wrote the music that is now regarded by many lovers of classical music as the greatest music ever written. Beethoven was born in 1770 in

Portrait of composer Ludwig van Beethoven holding a musical score

Bonn, where his grandfather had been a professional singer at the royal court. At only twelve years old, young Ludwig began to teach piano and participated in the musical life of the court. The Elector of Cologne sent Beethoven to Vienna when the musican was twenty-two. He worked there most of the remainder of his life. Soon after moving, he began to lose his hearing. Astonishingly, he heard his greatest works only in his head. He became most famous for his nine great symphonies, which are regarded as the core of every orchestra's repertoire. The city of Bonn holds a Beethoven festival in September and October each year.

Germany, Wagner, and Music

Composer Richard Wagner was born in Leipzig in 1813. He was fascinated by German folklore, especially the great Nibelung tales, which he turned into a series of grand operas.

In 1876, Wagner built an opera house in Bayreuth meant just for staging his Ring of the Nibelung cycle. Called the *Festspielhaus* ("Festival Playhouse"), Wagner's small opera house still hosts the Bayreuth Wagner Festival every summer. Opera fans come from all over the world for the performances.

Adolf Hitler, who was determined to bring all things German to the public attention, liked the anti-Semitic Wagner's music so much that he ordered orchestras made up of prisoners in concentration camps to play it. Even today, many Jews will not attend a concert if Wagner's music is to be played.

One of the inventors of modern classical music was Paul Hindemith, who was born in Hanau in 1895. He began playing

Opera fans congregate outside at the Bayreuth Wagner Festival.

Wagner and the Mad King's Castle

Castles should be old and alive with ancient fairy tales. Germany's most fairytale-like castle is Neuschwanstein, but it isn't very old. It was not built until the 1870s. It was constructed out of the top of a mountain as one of several castles planned by Bavarian king Ludwig II, who is often called the Mad King. Ludwig was a great fan of Wagner, and some of the rooms at Neuschwanstein are painted with scenes from Wagner's operas. In fact, it may be that he built the castle just to have a suitable place to put on productions of Wagner's opera *Tannhäuser*. Neuschwanstein was planned to have more than sixty rooms, but only fifteen had been constructed by the time of Ludwig's death.

professionally when he was eighteen, and his first composition was played in public two years later. After his unusual music was denounced by the Nazis in 1934, he spent little time in Germany. He and his wife, who was Jewish, finally moved to Switzerland in 1938. He spent most of the remainder of his life in the United States, becoming a U.S. citizen in 1946.

Popular Music

Most German young people find pop music much more interesting than that of the classical composers of their history. German industry has gone international and so has German music.

A group called the Scorpions was formed in Hanover in 1969. Though the group's performers have changed over the years, they are still recording hits. They are quite popular throughout Europe.

A heavy-metal band called Rammstein was formed in East Berlin in 1993. The group made several albums that, despite being sung in German, reached major sales in the United States and Britain. It's been said that they named themselves after the town where a 1988 air-show disaster killed many people.

The popular hip-hop group called The Fantastic Four began in Stuttgart in 1990. By 2000, they had had so many hits that they had started book and music publishing businesses. They also sponsor the Hip-Hop Open each year, a music festival for charity.

Golden Literature

At the heart of German literature is Johann Wolfgang von Goethe. He was born in Frankfurt am Main in 1749. Trained as a lawyer, he was most interested in philosophy, nature,

Rock group Rammstein

and history. Goethe is most famous for his long drama in poetry that tells the story of Faust, who sells his soul to the devil, Mephistopheles, in order to gain complete knowledge. The devil loses because Faust continually seeks perfection, which is a trait of godliness, not evil.

The Brothers Grimm

Jakob and Wilhelm Grimm, who were natives of Hanau, collected tales and folk poetry and published many of them in *Children's and Household Tales*. Their versions of these tales are the ones we know best today. They include the stories of Cinderella, Bremen Town Musicians, Tom Thumb, the Goose Girl, Snow White, Rapunzel, and Sleeping Beauty. The Grimm brothers were part of the movement that was trying to create a German nation. Because of that focus, they also developed a historical dictionary of the German language. They lived most of their lives in Kassel.

By contrast, Karl May, a writer in the late nineteenth century, popularized American westerns in Germany. He wrote many books in a series about Winnetou, a great Apache warrior. May got the idea for his books from attending a Buffalo Bill Cody Wild West Show in Germany in 1889. Called the most-read German author of all time, he was born in Hohenstein-Ernstthal and lived his whole life in Saxony.

He Went Home

Unlike most people who were forced to leave Germany in the years before the war, playwright Bertolt Brecht spent the war years in the United States and then went to Switzerland in 1948, then to East Germany in 1949 where he remained. In East Berlin, Brecht, who was born in Augsburg, ran a small theater called Berlin Ensemble. Today, the region around the theater is Bertolt Brecht Plaza. Among his most famous plays are *The Threepenny Opera* (which German composer Kurt Weill set to music that includes the famous "Mack the Knife") and *Mother Courage and Her Children*. He died in 1956. His plays are performed the world over.

Twentieth-Century Nobel Writers

Many German writers have won the Nobel Prize for Literature, an important international award.

1999—Günter Grass was born in Danzig, where his novel *The Tin Drum* takes place.

1972—Heinrich Böll, a native of Cologne, was credited with "renewing German literature."

1966—Nelly Sachs, a native of Berlin, was a poet who escaped to Sweden in 1940.

1946—Herman Hesse, born in the Black Forest, left Germany and became a Swiss citizen.

1929—Thomas Mann, born in Lübeck, is the author of *The Magic Mountain.*

1912—Playwright Gerhart Hauptmann was born in Bad Obersalzbrunn.

1910—Berlin-born Paul Heyse was famed for his novellas, or short novels.

1908—Born in Aurich, Rudolf Christoph Eucken wrote on philosophy.

1902—Christian Matthias Theodor Mommsen, of Schleswig, wrote on Roman history.

Sculptor Käthe Kollwitz created this work in memory of her son who died in World War I.

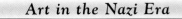

Art in the Nazi Era

It was difficult to be an artist with any individuality during the Nazi era in Germany. Many artists discovered early in the 1930s that it was probably time to leave, though others remained.

Sculptor and printmaker Käthe Kollwitz was born in East Prussia in 1867. She used her superb artistic skills to sketch scenes of poverty and war in stark black and white, then made fine prints of the pictures. One of her greatest sculptures is a war memorial to her son who died in World War I; her grandson died in World War II. Frowned on by the Nazis, her work was removed from German museums until after the war. There are Käthe Kollwitz Museums in Cologne and Berlin.

In 1919, in Weimar, a Berlin architect named Walter Gropius started an art academy named the Bauhaus. It was later closed by the Nazis, and one of Gropius's colleagues,

Mies van der Rohe, went to the United States. There he became famous for his rectangular buildings in which the structural steel was visible. Much of the famous "modern" design of the twentieth century, such as tubular chairs, stemmed from the Bauhaus.

A member of Germany's professional soccer team (center) was challenged by Finland during the World Cup qualifiers in 2001.

Soccer

Sports of all kinds are immensely popular in Germany. There are almost 80,000 sporting clubs of various sizes around the country. More than 5 million Germans belong to the German Soccer Federation. That means that 5 million people actively play and support soccer, at all levels from neighborhood pickup games to international competitions.

There are two professional soccer leagues that play throughout the country. West German national teams won the World Cup professional soccer matches in 1954, 1974, and 1990. Player Franz Beckenbauer is one of Germany's sports heroes.

In the 1999 Women's World Cup, the German soccer team reached the quarter-finals but lost to the United States, which went on to win the tournament.

In 2001, an immigrant from Ghana, Gerald Asamoah, became the first black, African-born player to wear the jersey of Germany's national soccer team. He had lived in Germany since he was twelve years old but became a German citizen just months before joining the team.

Throughout the forty years of the GDR, sports were used by the government as a way of giving East Germans a feeling of national identity. Sports activities, especially local clubs, were also used as a way of teaching communist ideas. Sports heroes made personal appearances at festivals, where thousands of people would see them and link them with the new "fatherland."

The Olympics

German teams have always scored well in Olympic competitions. The most infamous Olympics were Germany's own, the 1936 Summer Olympics in Berlin. A new stadium was built for those Olympics. Hitler was determined to show the world that the "pure Aryans" could beat everyone. And, indeed, Germany did win the most medals—eighty-nine, with thirty-three of them gold. But when it came to track and field

The cover of a German magazine celebrating the 1936 Olympics held in Berlin.

events, the star was African American runner Jesse Owens. He took gold medals in four events. It is said that Hitler, appalled at a black man beating his Aryans, refused to shake hands with Owens. Today, a street near the Olympic Stadium is named Jesse-Owens-Strasse in his honor. The stadium is being refurbished to make it useful as a sports arena in the twenty-first century.

The Winter Olympics that year (they were then held the same year as the Summer Olympics) were held at Garmisch-Partinkirchen in the Bavarian Alps. In those events, Germany came in second to Norway.

After the war, East Germany did not compete as a separate nation until 1968. That year, the two Germanies fielded two separate teams.

In the 1970s and 1980s, East Germany won almost 200 gold medals in the Olympic Games. The world was especially awestruck by the prowess of the East German swimmers. As the twenty-first century started, those same gold medal winners were suing the former sports authorities of the GDR. The former swimmers claimed that from earliest childhood they had secretly been given steroids and other muscle-building chemicals that are known to be very dangerous.

Individual Champions

In 1969 and 1970, East German figure skater Gabriele Seyfert was world champion. In 1974, both the men's and the women's figure-skating champions were from East Germany— Jan Hoffman and Christine Errath. Katarina Witt, also from

East Germany and now of New York, held the championship every year between 1983 and 1988. Witt also won two gold medals at the Winter Olympics.

Germans have also been important figures in international tennis. Steffi Graf, a champion in the 1980s and 1990s, is a native of Mannheim. She returned to Germany to concentrate on coaching junior girls in professional tennis. Boris Becker, born in Leiman, was, at seventeen, the youngest man to win the men's singles championship at Wimbledon in England in 1986.

Above left: **Katarina Witt at the 1994 Winter Olympics in Lillehammer**

Above right: **Tennis champion Steffi Graf**

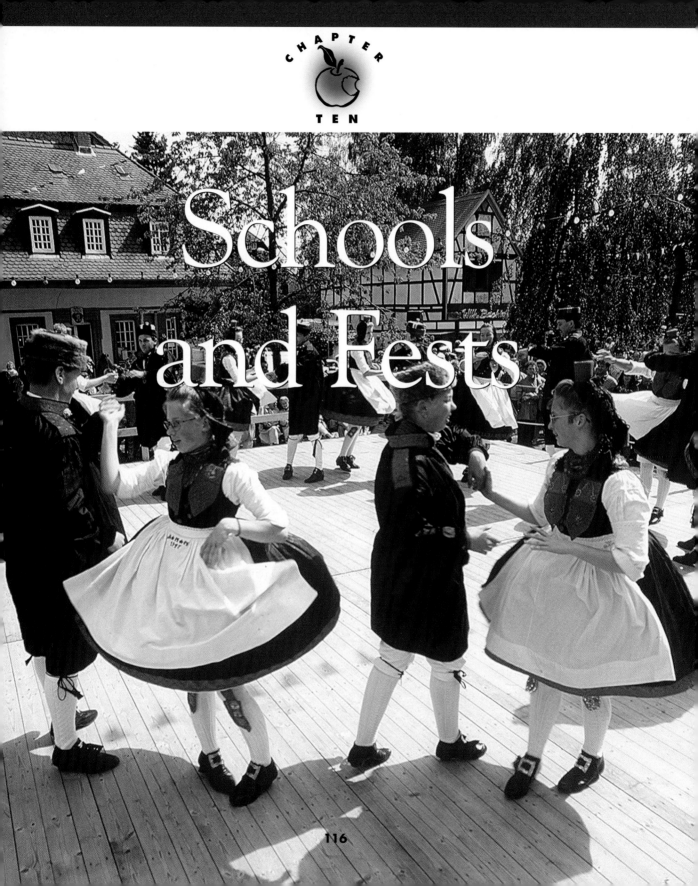

Schools and Fests

V ISITORS LOVE TO GO TO GERMANY BECAUSE IT'S "QUAINT," "beautiful," "historic," and more. To the Germans, it's home— the place where they go to school, work, play, and generally enjoy life.

Opposite: **Folk dancers perform at the Schwalmstadt Festival in Hessen.**

Little Children at School

Kindergarten started in Germany, where an educator named Friedrich Fröbel began this early education in Blankenburg in 1840. He invented the word *kindergarten*, meaning "garden of children," to imply an education gentler than "school." Twenty years after Fröbel started his school, a student of his, Margarethe Schurz, emigrated to the United States with her husband Carl. She began the first U.S. kindergarten in Watertown, Wisconsin, in 1853.

Kindergarten is not part of the standard German public school offerings. Parents have to pay to send their children to private kindergartens.

High school students can choose what type of school to attend.

Going to School in Germany

Public schools in the East and West were somewhat different in arrangement. When reunification occurred, the government decided to delay decisions on making education the same in all the Länder.

In general, children are required to attend school between the ages of six and fifteen. Elementary school, or *Grundschule*, covers ages six through ten (or until age twelve in Berlin). After that, students must choose between the academic (college-bound) *Gymnasium* and the vocational or job-oriented *Realschule*. A good student in *Realschule* can, on graduating at age sixteen, transfer to the *Gymnasium* for a further three years. A third type of high school is the *Hauptschule*, or general high school.

A diploma from this school, earned by the ninth or tenth grade, qualifies a student to go on to technical or clerical training.

Many Länder are building *Gesamtschulen,* or comprehensive schools. These high schools feature the same programs as all three other high schools. All schools require young people to study English and usually one other language, in addition to German.

Universities

In 2001, 1.8 million students attended German colleges and universities. About 10 percent of them were from other countries. For German citizens, most universities are free, though

University students relax between classes.

the students must pay their own living costs. There are 320 institutions of higher learning in Germany.

One of the oldest universities in the world is Charles University in Prague (now in the Czech Republic), where the German language was once used in all classes. It was established in 1348. Now, the largest German university is in Munich.

In the 1990s, only one out of every three students who tried to get into university was able to. Young people in the eastern Länder are less likely to go on to university than those in the western Länder, though this will gradually change. There are also fewer jobs in the East for those who don't go on to college.

Holidays and Festivals

Germans have at least ten official holidays, and some Länder offer even more. They are mostly related to religious life except for New Year's Day and Labor Day (called May Day in some countries). The newest holiday is October 3, Day of German Unity. This celebrates the day in 1990 that East and West Germany were once again a single, unified German nation.

The law requires twenty-four days of annual vacation for all employed people. Workers are also guaranteed paid leave to spend time at a health resort to recover from job stress.

Munich is known for probably the largest festival in Europe, Oktoberfest.

National Holidays in Germany

New Year's Day	January 1
Good Friday	March or April
Easter Sunday	March or April
Easter Monday	March or April
Ascension Thursday	May
Labor Day	May 1
Pentecost	Sunday in May or June
Whit Monday	Day after Pentecost in May or June
Day of German Unity	October 3
Christmas	December 25

It began in 1810 at the wedding of Ludwig I, king of Bavaria, to Princess Therese of Saxe-Hildburghausen. Since then, this autumn holiday has become a fun time in many countries of the world, before winter sets in. Almost 6 million people each year come to Munich for the festival, now best known for its beer. Some of the beer tents spaced around the city are large

Festival-goers fill a beer hall at Munich's Oktoberfest.

enough to hold 6,000 people at a time. German bands can be heard playing lively music called the polka.

Personal Life

For the most part, Germans dress like other Europeans and Americans. However, traditional clothing called *trachten* is worn for special events and festivals in some parts of the country. Much of what we think of as "typical German" trachten is actually from Bavaria. For the men, it consists of shorts called

Folk dancers perform in Germany's traditional dress.

EXPO 2000

The first world's fair ever held in Germany took place in Hanover in 2000. It had the theme "Humankind–Nature–Technology: A New World Arising." More than 800 exhibits and events from countries around the world were presented at the expo. They included everything from pop concerts to yachting exhibitions at nearby Wilhelmshaven to studies of "Living Lakes" to Chinese art. Hundreds of thousands of people from all over the world came to the fair. Hanover is used to fairs. The largest industrial fair in the world is held there each year.

lederhosen ("leather stockings") with embroidered suspenders and knee socks. The women wear full, gathered skirts called *dirndls*, usually with white blouses and embroidered belts.

At the turn of the twenty-first century, marriage generally occurred for women at age twenty-six and for men at twenty-nine. It had been earlier in the GDR, but since reunification, eastern Germans have also been marrying later.

Germans like to drive, and they like to drive fast. Big expressways, called *Autobahns*, crisscross the country, and there are few speed limits on them.

Trucks and cars speed along Germany's autobahns.

Although pizza, hamburgers (originally named for the town of Hamburg), and steak are popular food, Germany is best known for its sausages, called *wurst*. Making sausage was

This butcher is ready to sell you any of Germany's delicious wursts.

a way of preserving meat before refrigeration. Meat of various kinds would be chopped up and mixed with spices, then stuffed into casings. Both the name *sausage* and *salami* (a kind of hard sausage) come from the Latin word for salt.

In Germany every region had its own way of making sausage. There are still hundreds of kinds. Many of them were brought to the United States by German immigrants. The frankfurter was a sausage developed in Frankfurt. Braunschweiger is a spreadable sausage from Braunschweig, near Hanover.

There are 1,200 breweries (beer-making establishments) in Germany. One at Weihenstephen dates back to the eleventh century. German beer halls are much larger than British pubs or American bars. They may seat hundreds of people. Beer gardens are another place to enjoy good food and German brews in an outdoor setting.

Regular nightclubs are popular, too, especially in the big cities. The nightclubs of Hamburg attracted some young musicians from Liverpool, England, in about 1960. After they returned to England, they linked up with a new drummer and formed a group that became known as the Beatles.

Germany is an exciting mix of past and future. Germany is eager to welcome the world, to show where it has been and to experience what it is becoming.

Timeline

German History

	About
People are moving into Germany.	500 B.C.
Prince Arminius defeats the Romans near Bielefeld.	A.D. 9
Charlemagne, king of the Franks, brings many German states into his kingdom.	770s
Munich is founded.	1158
German cities form the Hanseatic League.	1241
Johannes Gutenberg uses the first movable type to print a book, the Bible.	1456
Martin Luther's conflict with the Catholic Church starts the Protestant Reformation in Germany.	1517
The Thirty Years' War.	1618–1648
Thirty-five German-speaking states are loosely united in the Peace of Westphalia.	1648
Thirty-four German states join as the Confederation of the Rhine.	1806–1813
More than forty German states are loosely united in the German Confederation.	1815
Uprisings occur but fail to create a republic.	1848
Otto von Bismarck of Prussia sets up the North German Confederation.	1867

World History

2500 B.C.	Egyptians build the Pyramids and the Sphinx in Giza.
563 B.C.	The Buddha is born in India.
A.D. 313	The Roman emperor Constantine recognizes Christianity.
610	The Prophet Muhammad begins preaching a new religion called Islam.
1054	The Eastern (Orthodox) and Western (Roman) Churches break apart.
1066	William the Conqueror defeats the English in the Battle of Hastings.
1095	Pope Urban II proclaims the First Crusade.
1215	King John seals the Magna Carta.
1300s	The Renaissance begins in Italy.
1347	The Black Death sweeps through Europe.
1453	Ottoman Turks capture Constantinople, conquering the Byzantine Empire.
1492	Columbus arrives in North America.
1500s	The Reformation leads to the birth of Protestantism.
1776	The Declaration of Independence is signed.
1789	The French Revolution begins.
1865	The American Civil War ends.

German History

The confederation is joined by states in southern Germany to form the German Empire.	1871
Germany enters the Great War.	1914
Germany admits defeat and surrenders, ending World War I; the Weimar Republic is formed.	1918
Adolf Hitler writes *Mein Kampf*.	1925
The Nazi Party gains a majority in parliament.	1932
Hitler becomes chancellor of Germany; the Reichstag is burned.	1933
Hitler declares himself the leader of the Third Reich.	1934
Germany hosts the Olympics.	1936
Germany invades Poland, starting World War II.	1939
Hitler commits suicide and Germany surrenders, ending World War II in Europe; Germany is divided into four sectors.	1945
The Soviet Union tries to blockade Berlin but the United States organizes an airlift.	1948
Western Germany becomes the Federal Republic of Germany; eastern Germany becomes the German Democratic Republic.	1949
West Germany is rebuilt.	1950s
West Germany becomes a founding member of the European Economic Community.	1957
East Germany builds the Berlin Wall.	1961
Chancellor Willy Brandt of West Germany works to improve relations with East Germany and eastern Europe.	1969–1974
West Germany's Green Party becomes the leading group in Europe for saving the environment.	1980s
The Berlin Wall is torn down.	1989
Germany is reunited.	1990
Berlin is named the capital of the reunified Germany.	1991
Germany signs the Maastricht Treaty establishing the European Union.	1992
The euro becomes the official currency of Germany	2002

World History

1914	World War I breaks out.
1917	The Bolshevik Revolution brings communism to Russia.
1929	Worldwide economic depression begins.
1939	World War II begins, following the German invasion of Poland.
1945	World War II ends.
1957	The Vietnam War starts.
1969	Humans land on the moon.
1975	The Vietnam War ends.
1979	Soviet Union invades Afghanistan.
1983	Drought and famine in Africa.
1989	The Berlin Wall is torn down, as communism crumbles in Eastern Europe.
1991	Soviet Union breaks into separate states.
1992	Bill Clinton is elected U.S. president.
2000	George W. Bush is elected U.S. president.

Fast Facts

Official name: Federal Republic of Germany

Capital: Berlin

Official language: German

Frankfurt

Germany's flag

Bavaria

Official religion:	None
Year of founding:	1949, West Germany; 1990 reunification of East Germany and West Germany
National anthem:	*Deutschlandlied* ("Song of Germany")
Government:	Federal republic
Chief of state:	President
Head of government:	Chancellor
Area and dimensions:	137,846 square miles (356,994 sq km)
Distance North to South:	540 miles (876 km)
Distance East to West:	398 miles (641 km)
Latitude and longitude of geographic center:	51° North, 9° East
Borders:	North Sea, Denmark, and Baltic Sea to the north; Poland and Czech Republic to the east; Austria and Switzerland to the south; France, Luxembourg, Belgium, and the Netherlands to the west
Highest elevation:	Zugspitze, 9,721 feet (2,963 m) above sea level
Lowest elevation:	Freepsum Lake, 6.5 feet (2 m) below sea level
Average temperature:	21°F (–6°C) in the mountains to 35°F (1°C) in the lowlands, in January; 64°F (17.8°C) in the lowlands to 68°F (20°C) in the southern valleys
Average precipitation:	From 20 to 28 inches (51 to 71 cm) in the northern lowlands to 80 inches (203 cm) in the Bavarian Alps

Neuschwanstein Castle

National population (2001 est.): 83,029,536

Population of largest cities (2000 est.):

Berlin (2001 est.)	3,458,763
Hamburg	1,707,986
Munich	1,225,809
Cologne	964,346
Frankfurt	647,304

Famous landmarks:

▶ *Berchtesgaden National Park*, near Austrian border

▶ *Black Forest*, southwestern Germany

▶ *Deutsches Museum*, Munich

▶ *Gemäldegalerie* (art museum), Berlin

▶ *Gutenberg Museum*, Mainz

▶ *Heidelberg Castle*, Heidelberg

▶ *Lorelei Rock*, on the Rhine River

▶ *Neuschwanstein Castle*, Füssen

▶ *Zwinger Museum and Gardens*, Dresden

Industry: Iron and steel production are important industries. Much of the steel is used to make automobiles, trucks, and ships, as well as machines and tools. Other important manufactured products include cement, electrical equipment, metals, computers, cameras, clothing, leather goods, and processed foods. Germany's main mining products include coal, potash, and rock salt. Large deposits of lignite coal are found in eastern Germany.

Currency: The euro. In July 2002, U.S.$1 = 1.01 euros.

System of weights and measures: Metric system

Currency

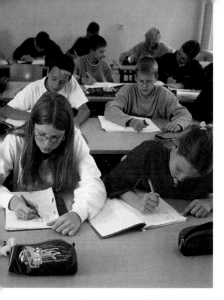

High school students

Literacy (1998 est.): 99 percent

Common German words and phrases:

Achtung! (AHK-tung)	Look out!
Auf Wiedersehen. (auf VEE-der-zane)	Good-bye.
Bitte (BIT-uh)	Please
Danke. (DAHN-kuh)	Thank you.
Guten Tag. (GOO-ten tahk)	Good day.
Ich heifse . . . (ich HI-suh)	My name is . . .
Ja (yah)	Yes
Nein (nine)	No
Wo ist . . .? (VO ist)	Where is . . . ?

Famous Germans:

Konrad Adenauer *Chancellor of West Germany*	(1876–1967)
Johann Sebastian Bach *Composer*	(1685–1750)
Ludwig van Beethoven *Composer*	(1770–1827)
Willy Brandt *Chancellor of West Germany*	(1913–1992)
Jacob Grimm	(1785–1863)
Wilhelm Grimm *Brothers who collected fairy tales*	(1786–1859)
Johann Wolfgang von Goethe *Poet*	(1749–1832)
George Frideric Handel *Composer*	(1685–1759)

Johann Sebastian Bach

To Find Out More

Nonfiction

▶ Bachrach, Susan D. *The Nazi Olympics: Berlin 1936*. Boston: Little Brown, 2000.

▶ Bradley, John and Catherine. *Germany: The Reunification of a Nation*. Hotspots series. New York: Gloucester Press, 1992.

▶ Fuller, Barbara. *Germany*. Cultures of the World series. Tarrytown, N.Y.: Marshall Cavendish, 1994.

▶ Grant, R. G. *The Berlin Wall*. New Perspectives series. Austin, Tex: Raintree Steck-Vaughn, 1999.

▶ Hinds, Kathryn. *The Cathedral*. Life in the Middle Ages series. Tarrytown, N.Y.: Benchmark Books, 2000.

▶ Holmes, Burton, et al. *Berlin*. The World 100 Years Ago series. Broomall, Pa.: Chelsea House, 1998.

▶ McGowen, Tom. *Frederick the Great, Bismarck, and the Unification of Germany*. In World History. Berkeley Heights, N.J.: Enslow, 2002.

▶ Pollard, Michael. *The Rhine*. Great Rivers series. Tarrytown, N.Y.: Benchmark Books, 1997

Biographies

▶ Emmerich, Elspeth, with Robert Hull. *My Childhood in Nazi Germany*. New York: Bookwright Press, 1991.

▶ Frank, Anne. *Anne Frank: The Diary of a Young Girl*. New York: Doubleday, 1959.

Fiction

▶ Owens, Lily, Ed. *The Complete Brothers Grimm Fairy Tales*. New York: Grammercy, 1993.

Videos

▶ *Berlin* (Super Cities). International Video Network, 1995.

▶ *Germany: Berlin and Bavaria and Beyond* (2-tape set). Channel 1000, 1996.

▶ *Schindler: His Story as Told by the Actual People He Saved*. Thames Video Collection.

Web Site

▶ **Welcome to Germany Info**
www.germany-info.org
Web site of the German Embassy in Washington, D.C.

Organizations and Embassies

▶ **German Embassy**
4645 Reservoir Road, NW
Washington, DC 20007

▶ **German Information Center**
871 United Nations Plaza
New York, NY 10017
gic1@germany-info.org.

Index

Page numbers in *italics* indicate illustrations.

Meet the Author

J EAN F. BLASHFIELD delights in learning lots of fascinating, though not always important, things about places and the people who live in them. She says that when writing a book for young people, she's often as challenged by what to leave *out* of the book as by what to put in.

She has been a traveler since she first went on a college choir tour of Europe. It included several stops in Germany, including an unplanned one at a beer hall in Munich, where the choir served as the entertainment.

She made up her mind that she would go back to Europe—not to sing, but for the sheer beauty, excitement, and history. After developing the *Young People's Science Encyclopedia* for Children's Press, she kept that promise to herself and returned to London to live. That city became her headquarters for three years of travel throughout Europe. It was in London that she first began to write books for young people.

Since then she has returned to Europe often (but not often enough! she says), while writing almost 100 books, most of them for young people. She likes best to write about interesting

places, but she loves history and science, too. In fact, one of her big advantages as a writer is that she becomes fascinated by just about every subject she investigates. She has created an encyclopedia of aviation and space, written popular books on murderers and houseplants, and had a lot of fun creating an early book on the things women have done, called *Hellraisers, Heroines, and Holy Women*.

She was the founder of the *Dungeons & Dragons* book department at TSR Inc. and became avidly interested in medieval history. She finds the ancient German gods and goddesses—and all their shenanigans—particularly enchanting.

Jean Blashfield was born in Madison, Wisconsin, and has lived in many other places. She graduated from the University of Michigan and worked for publishers in Chicago and Washington, D.C. She returned to the Lake Geneva area in southern Wisconsin when she married Wallace Black (a publisher, writer, and pilot) and began to raise a family. She has two grown children, three cats, and two computers in her Victorian home in Delavan. In addition to researching via her computers, she produces whole books on the computer—scanning pictures, creating layouts, and even developing the index. She has become an ardent Internet surfer and is working on her own Web site, but she'll never give up her trips to the library—and to other countries.

Photo Credits